coloring FOR THE stressed out Modernist

a cool, calming coloring book of modern design for adults

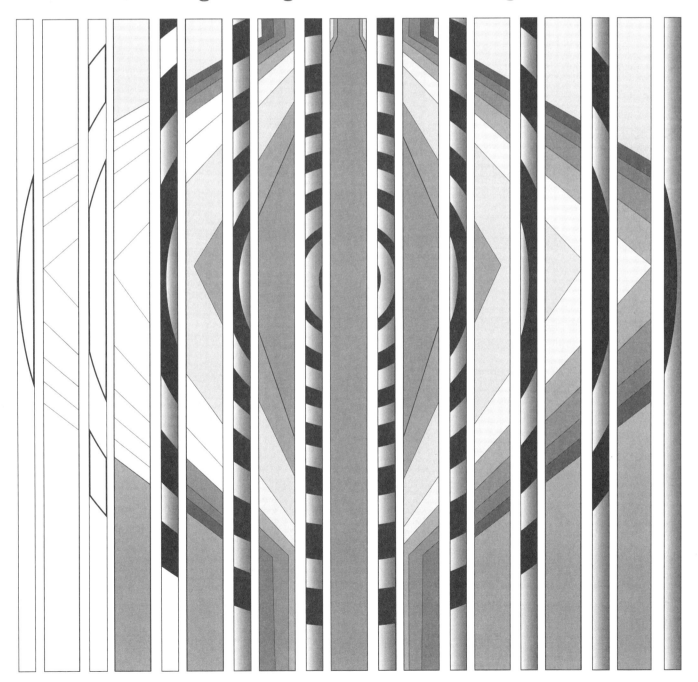

JENNIFER ZIMMERMANN

A POST HILL PRESS BOOK

ISBN: 978-1-68261-101-2

COLORING ZEN FOR THE STRESSED OUT MODERNIST
© 2016 by Jennifer Zimmermann
All Rights Reserved

No part of this book may be reproduced, stored in a retrieval system,
or transmitted by any means without the written permission of the author and publisher.

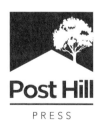

Post Hill Press
275 Madison Avenue, 14th Floor
New York, NY 10016
posthillpress.com

INTRO

In this modern day and age, stress is a factor in everyone's lives.

Everyone is in a rush to get somewhere, multitasking in the process, and every day is Groundhog's Day – yet our internal batteries are never fully charged and our caches aren't cleared. The abundance of technology at our fingertips makes tighter deadlines possible. Instant gratification is the way of the world, and like it or not, we are all caught up in the race to satisfy the next information download. We are addicted to our tablets and phones and can't function without them. We have forgotten how to live simply and take time for ourselves.

Recently, the scientific community has recognized the role that coloring can play as a supplement to therapy, almost meditative in process for some, in stress-relief and improved mental health. Coloring is a means to unlock our creative potential, clear our minds and zap anxiety all at once. Finding a balance of body, mind and spirit through coloring is easy because it doesn't require a battery or a connection. Coloring can change your state of mind and lift your spirit. Coloring is oftentimes a solo activity done in a quiet space. However, coloring books have also become a trendy pastime at adult dinner parties and bar meet-ups. This great social activity is a natural means to connect people with common interests. Visit **www.moderncoloring.com** to learn how to join or create a coloring meet-up, download colored reference images, or share your own colored pages.

Coloring Zen for the Stressed Out Modernist was designed to provide entertainment, whether solo or social. The goal was to create a zen, meditative-like space for the modern art enthusiast (or for people drawn to eye-catching images) – to provide an outlet for relaxation and unwinding – or just to have fun. It also serves a secondary purpose: these uniquely finished pieces of Modern Art can be proudly displayed in your home or office. Many of these images will also appeal to mid-century modern collectors and fans and make great gifts when framed. Modernists tend to be introspective perfectionists. They appreciate simple shapes and clean lines over the fussy and frilly, which also appeal to a variety of people, including most men. Because many of the designs in this book are not overly ornate, the colorist is able to keep them as simple or elaborate as desired. The lines are simply "guides" to contain your colors or embellishments. The end result is entirely original. The degree of difficulty varies from page to page, so decide which pages best suit you on a given day.

Modern Art itself is comprised of many movements. *Coloring Zen for the Stressed Out Modernist* was inspired by many, several of which are: Precisionism, Art Deco, Cubism, Minimalism, Hard Edge Painting, Op Art, and Color Field Painting to name a few. Much of the art from these periods is not narrative, but rather focuses on the process of creation itself, the artist's state of mind at the time of creation, and a great deal of experimentation. The beauty of the interaction between the elements on the canvas becomes much of the storyline. A good deal of mid-century art is abstract, non-representational or made up of simplified forms and patterns.

This book is a marriage of therapeutic exercises and art appreciation with many of the images being inspired by the art and design of the middle of the 20th century.

TIPS & TRICKS

Being a professional artist and art educator has helped in designing a coloring book. After spending many years learning and teaching best practices and techniques, it is easy to recommended some tried and true methods. As you relax and get situated to begin this coloring journey, it is important to keep a few things in mind:

Color is a huge component of most Modern Art. Adding color is vital to the success of your pages – these images will come to life when you do. Until then you may not realize their full potential. Peruse the online gallery for ideas.

Prepping
Before starting, choose and have readily available the most fitting coloring tools for each image as well as a comfortable place to color — then the focus can just be on relaxing and experiencing the zen that will come about.

Experiment
It may be helpful to use the last pages in the book allotted for practice and doodling. At first, it is important to pay attention to the way each material glides across the paper in this book. They will all feel different. After some trial and error, you should begin to recognize how each affects the paper and particular design. You may need to use short, swift movements or long, gradual strokes, depending on the size and shape of the part being colored and the chosen coloring tool. Either way, repetitive motions are relaxing and the more practice one gets, the better it will look…not to mention the benefits of improved hand-eye coordination. Colorists are encouraged to determine what works best, based on physical ability, fine motor coordination, age and skill. Some designs have larger, more vast spaces that would best be filled with a bold marker. Others have much smaller detail, so a thin marker, gel pen or very sharp colored pencil may do the trick. Keep a quality sharpener handy.

Avoid leaks
Always place a piece of freezer paper (plastic coated), chipboard or a few spare sheets of paper behind each coloring page that you attempt to use marker or any kind of water based writing utensil on. Every brand of marker responds differently to each paper type, and some may bleed, so better to

be safe than sorry. Try using your marker in the direction of the lines containing each shape, instead of randomly filling in from all angles. It will look neater and you won't destroy the "tooth" of the paper by overlapping too many times.

Tool and Technique Selection

There are a variety of illustrations, simple and complex, that require the use of different fine art utensils to best cover the shapes. Some spaces are very small, while others are vast. Use the appropriate tool for the job. For example, don't use a sharp colored pencil to fill in a large space that could be more easily filled with a thick marker or crayon. It will take a lot longer and it won't necessarily look better.

Choosing Quality Utensils

Not all crayons and colored pencils are created equally! My personal recommendation is old school Prismacolor and Verithin pencils. Using a light hand always helps too. If you are interested in finding out more, there are many blogs on coloring and a lot of information on the newest pencils, pens and markers colorists are recommending.

Coloring Effects

You may choose to color the images with solid color or add gradations (shading) if you desire. It is always recommended that if you plan to shade, you start with the lightest colors and work your way to the darkest, as most of the mediums you will likely use aren't erasable and are semi-opaque. It is possible to color in marker and add colored pencil details after the marker is completely dry. Many colorists love gel pens and glitter pens. It is all personal preference.

What colors should you use? Check out the online gallery for ideas. Different color schemes have different purposes. Complementary colors are attention grabbing and will make your image pop to give it that wow factor. Analogous colors (closely related such as blue-violet, violet, red-violet) are more harmonious, soothing and pleasurable to look at. Cool colors (greens, blues) are calming when used alone, and when used alongside warm colors will make objects appear to recede. Warm colors alone can look very cheerful and inviting. Many other detailed tips about coloring effects are available on the **www.moderncoloring.com.**

Page Removal

It would be best to use a utility knife and straight edge close to the binding of the page needing removal. A piece of chipboard or cardboard placed underneath the image will protect the pages below. Colorists may be inspired to remove their favorite finished pages to frame and hang these pieces in their own modern homes.

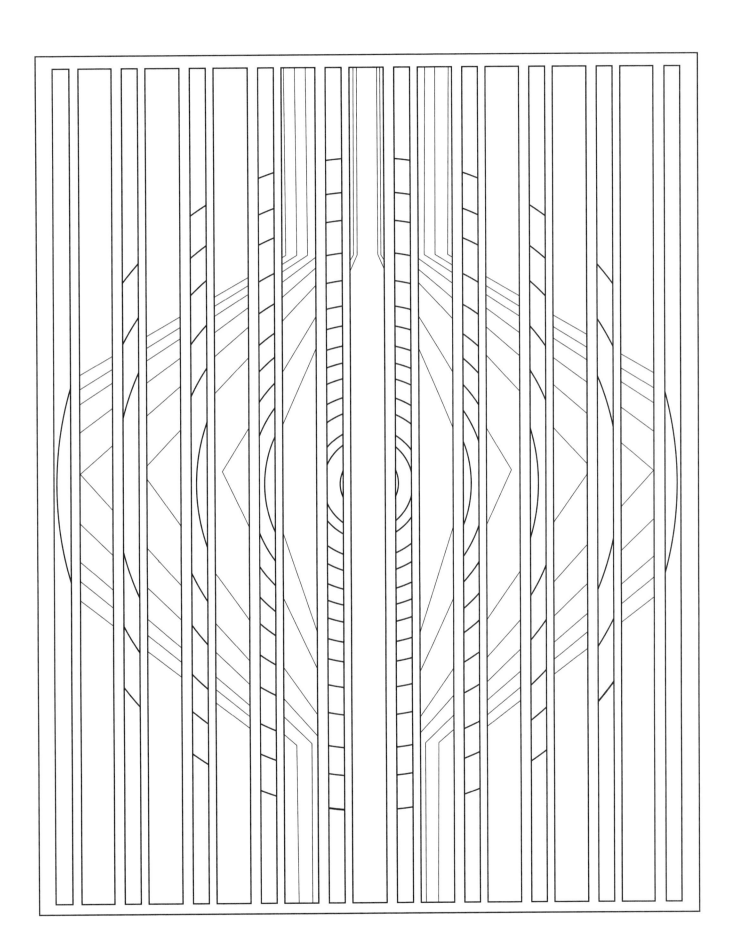

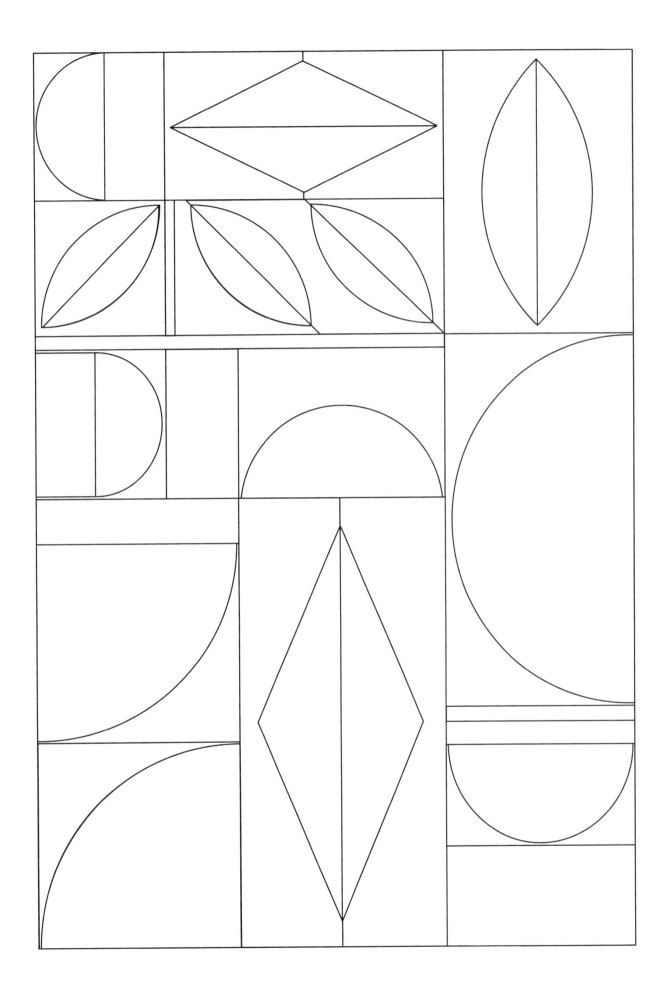

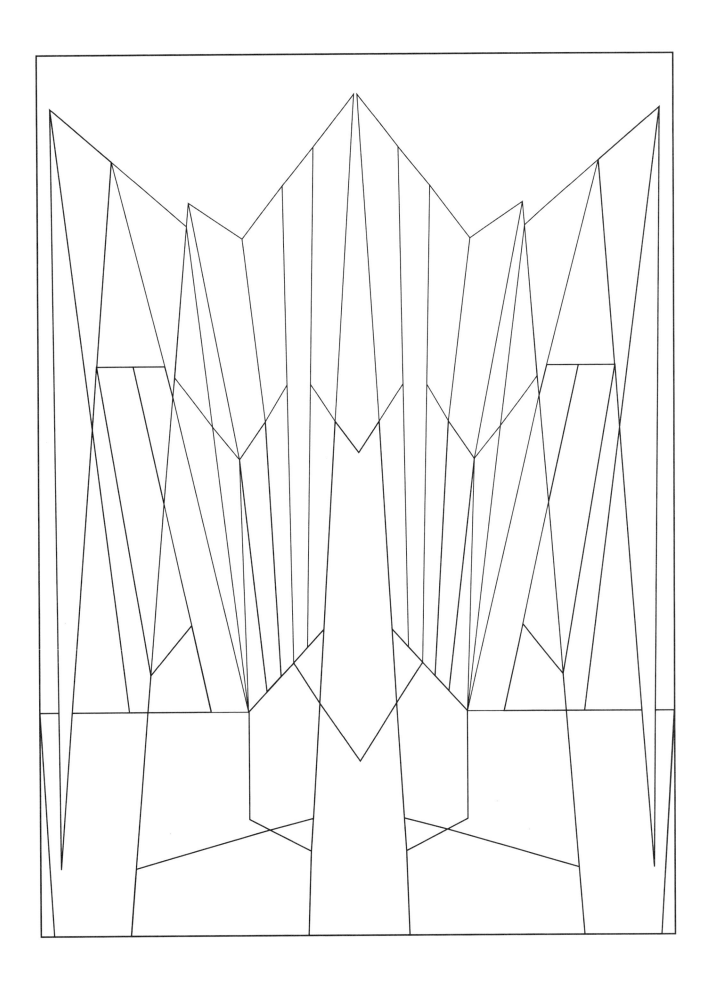

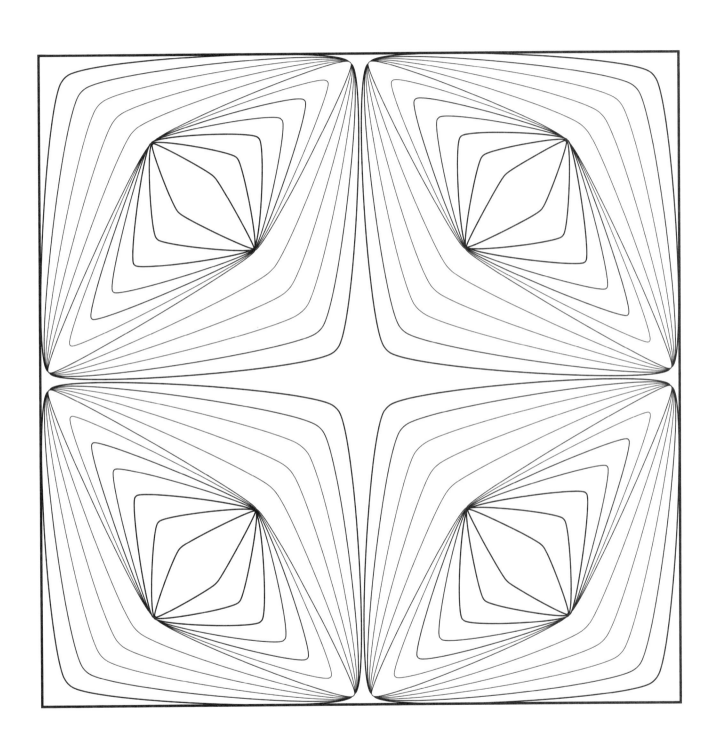

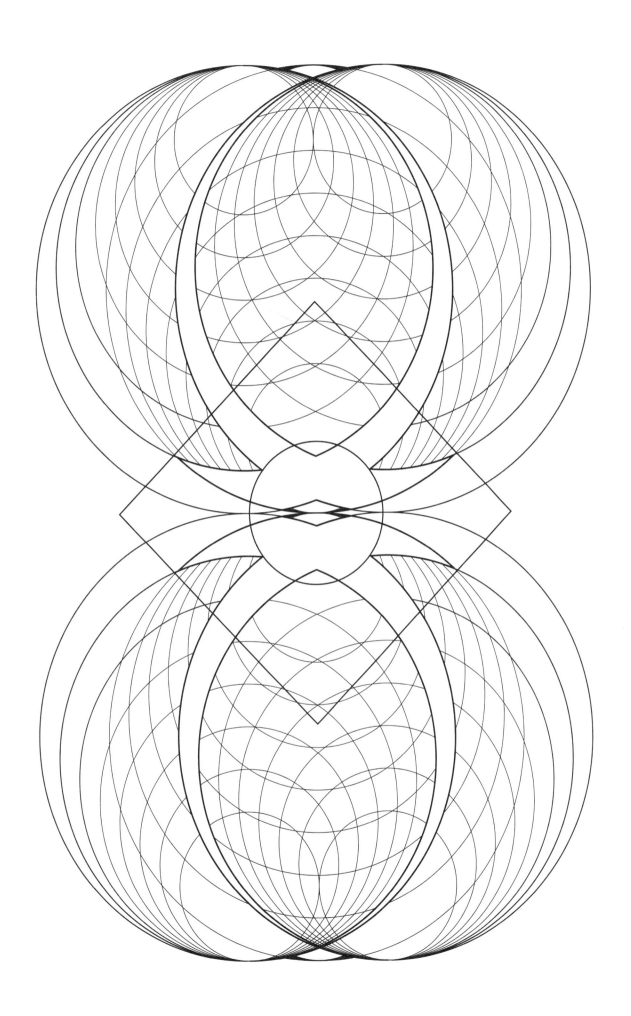

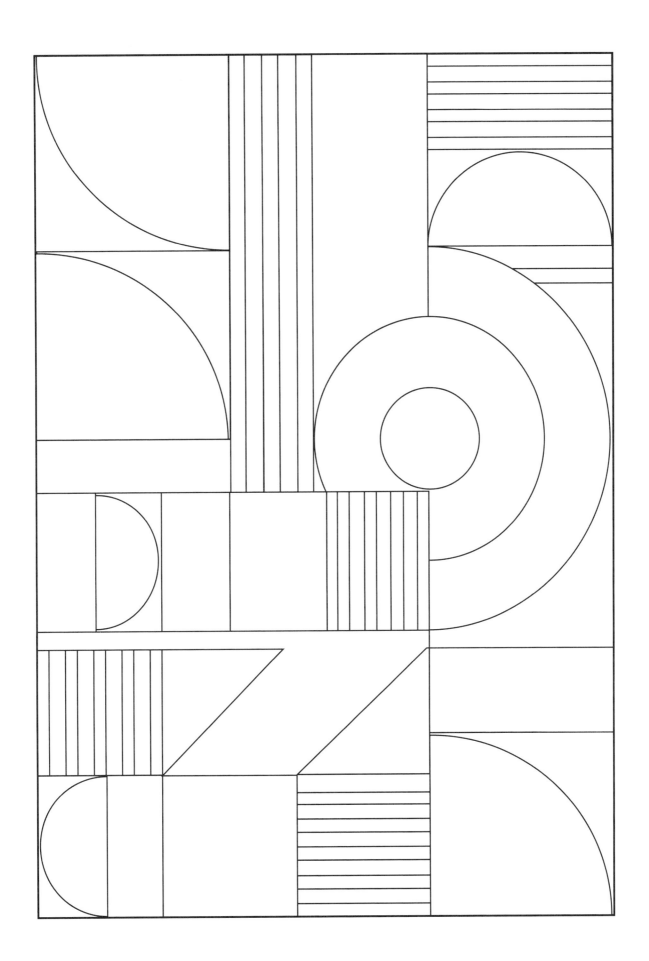

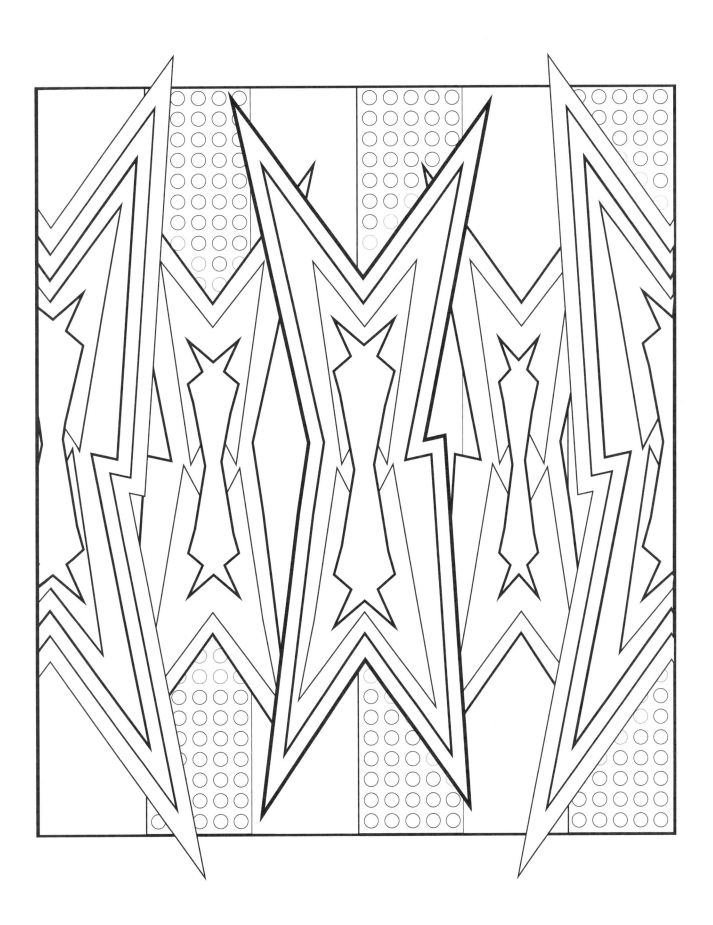

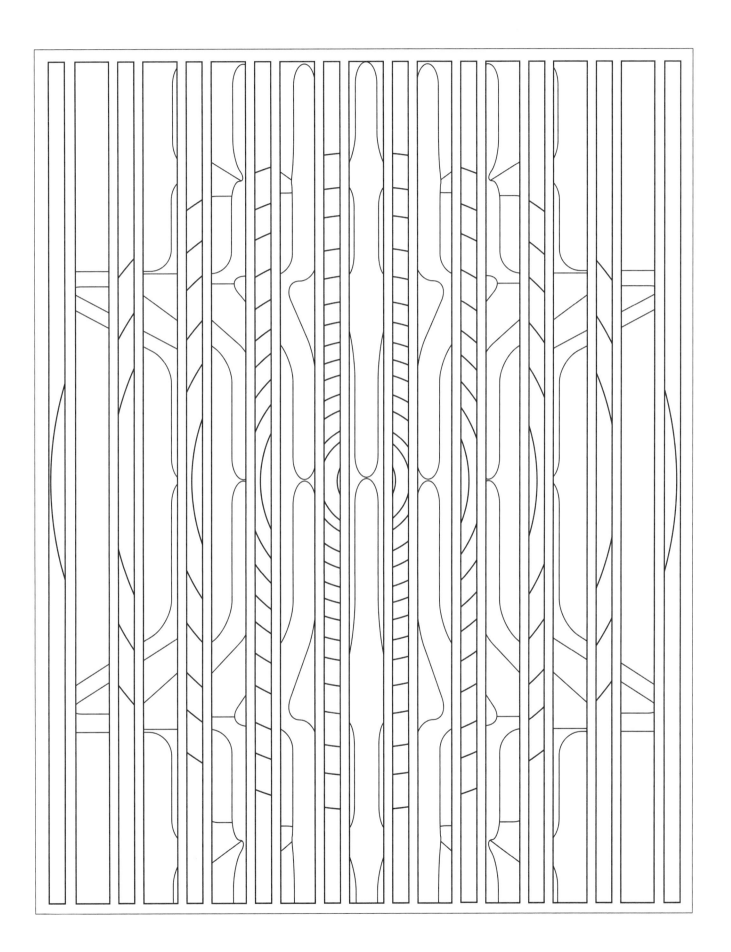

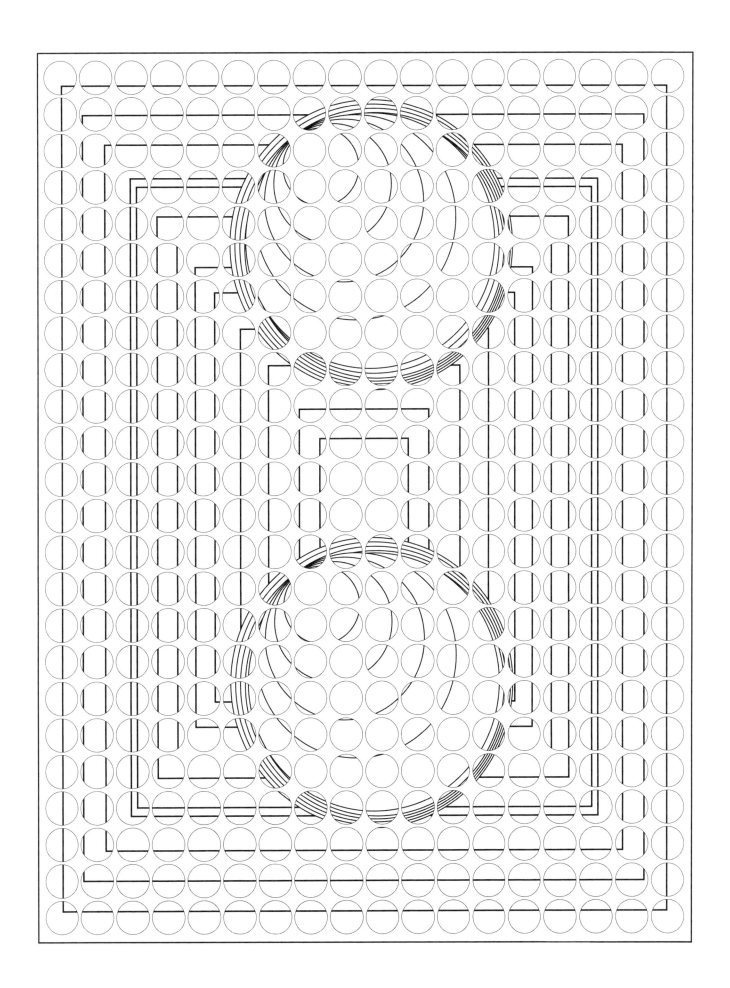

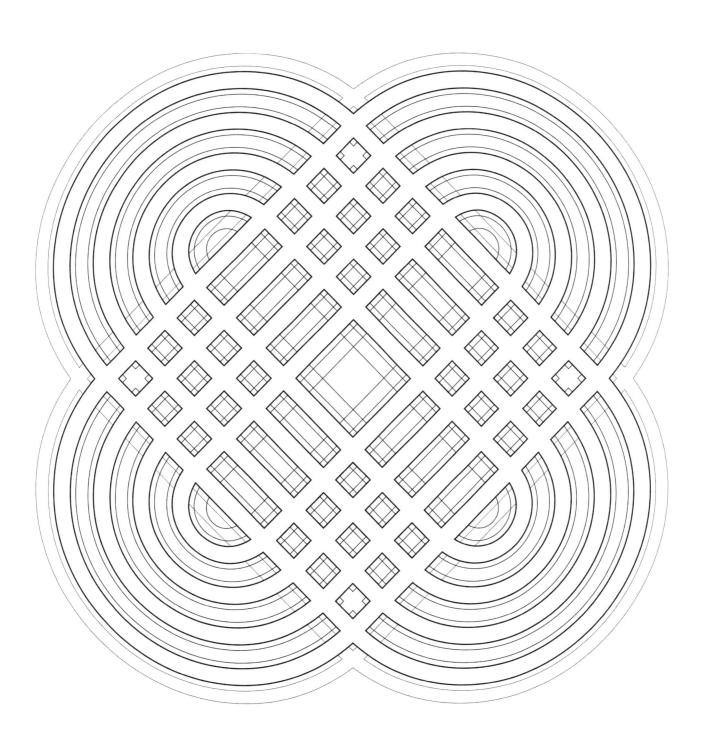

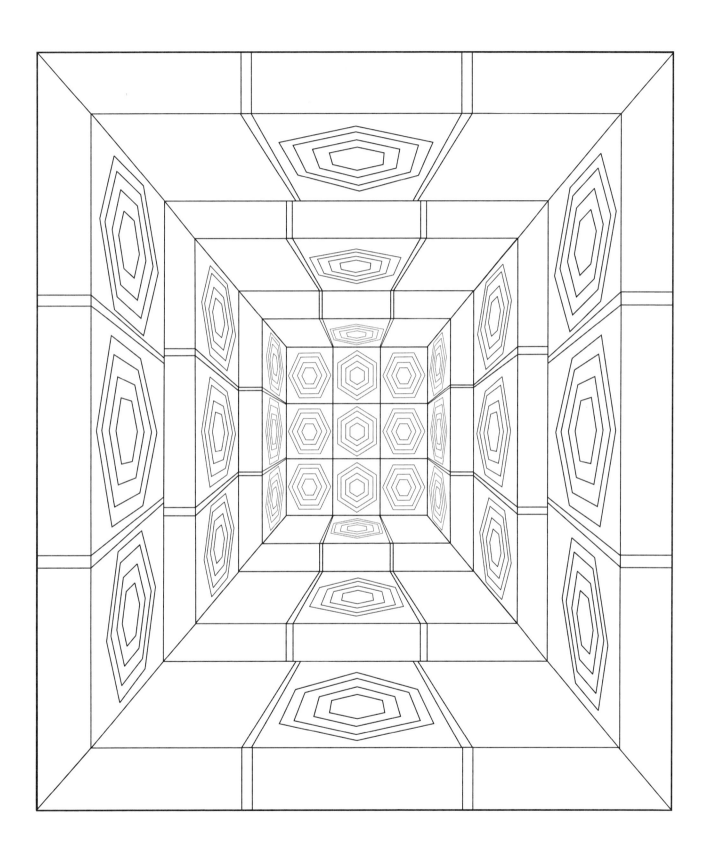

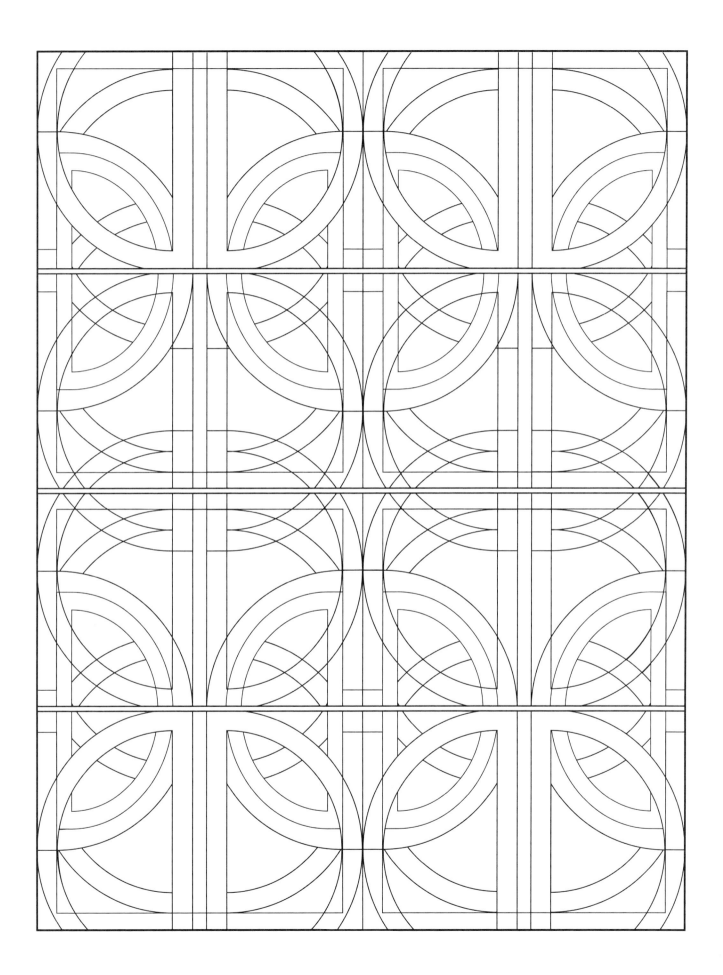

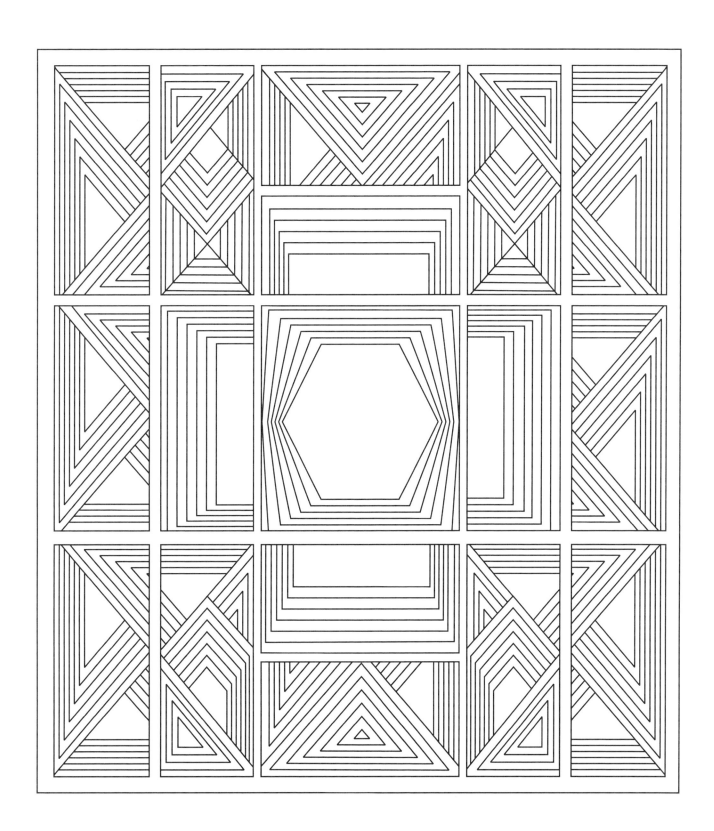

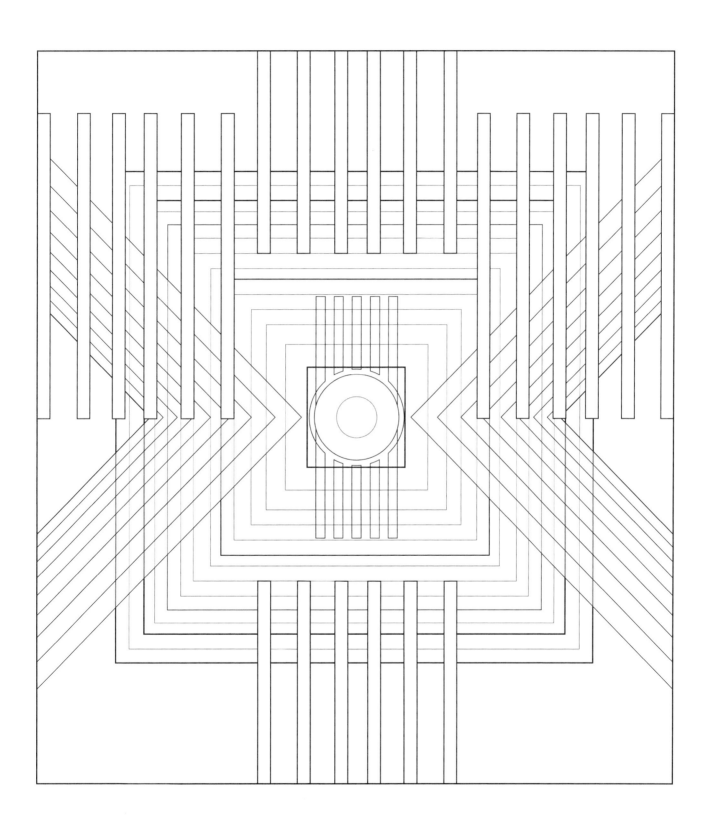

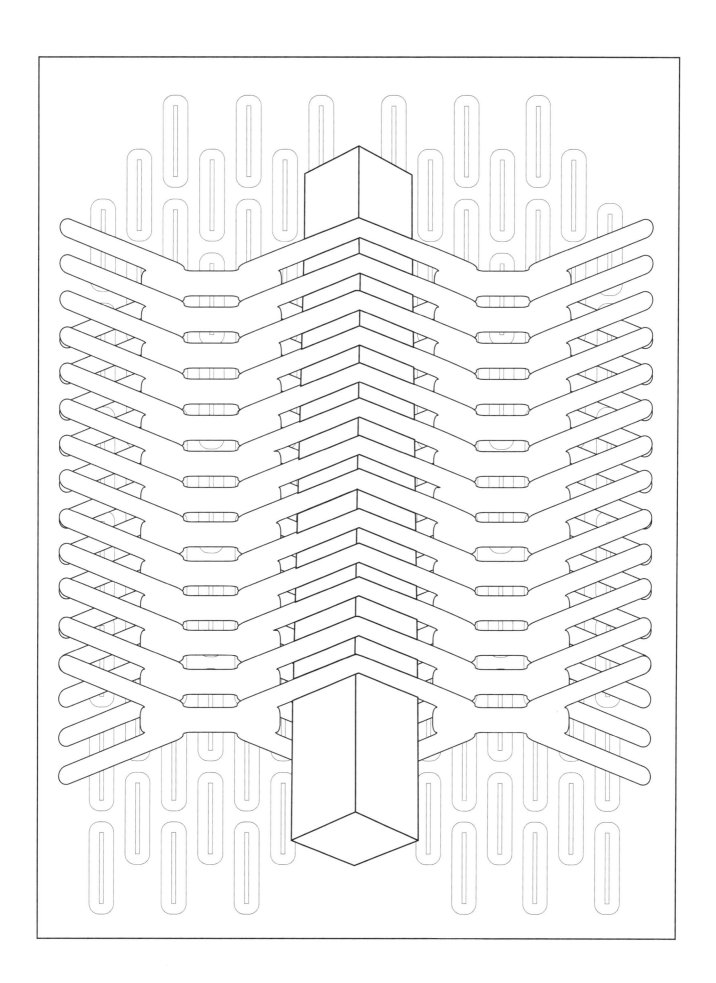

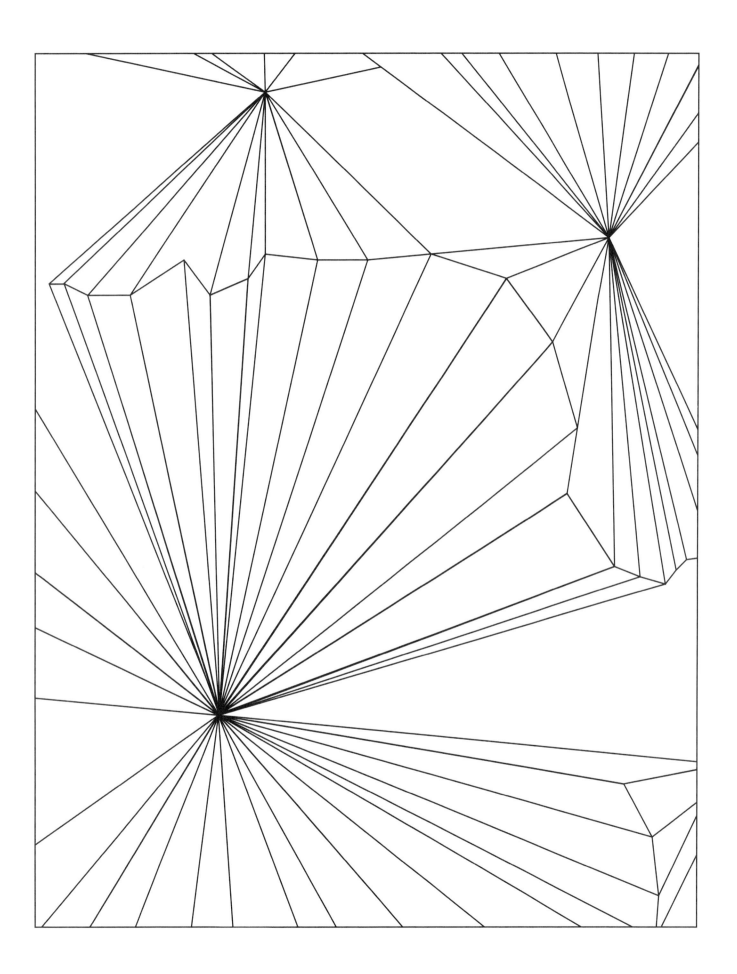

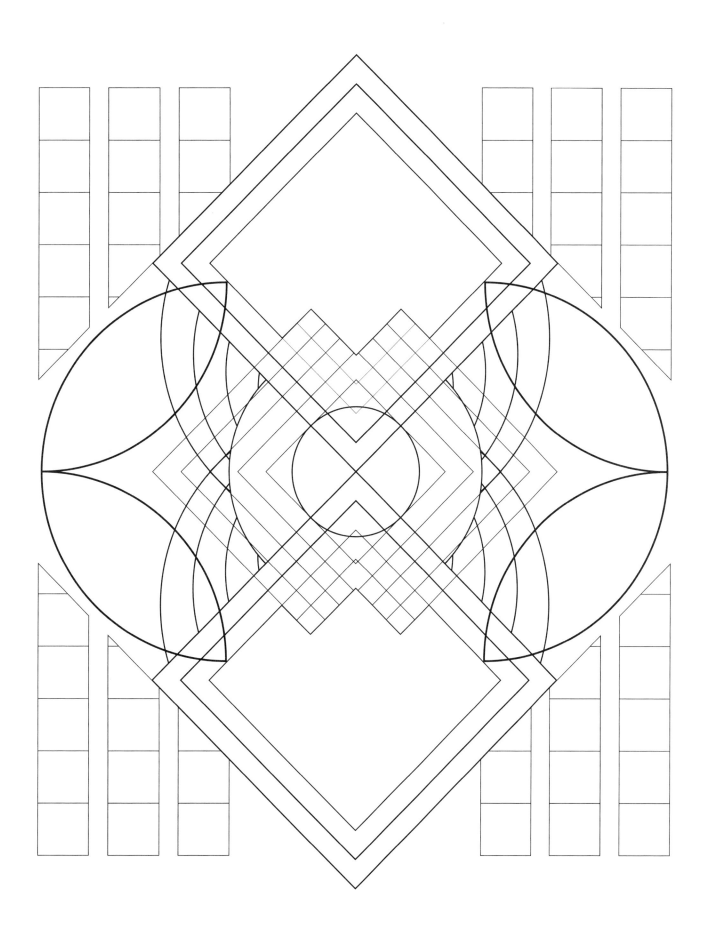

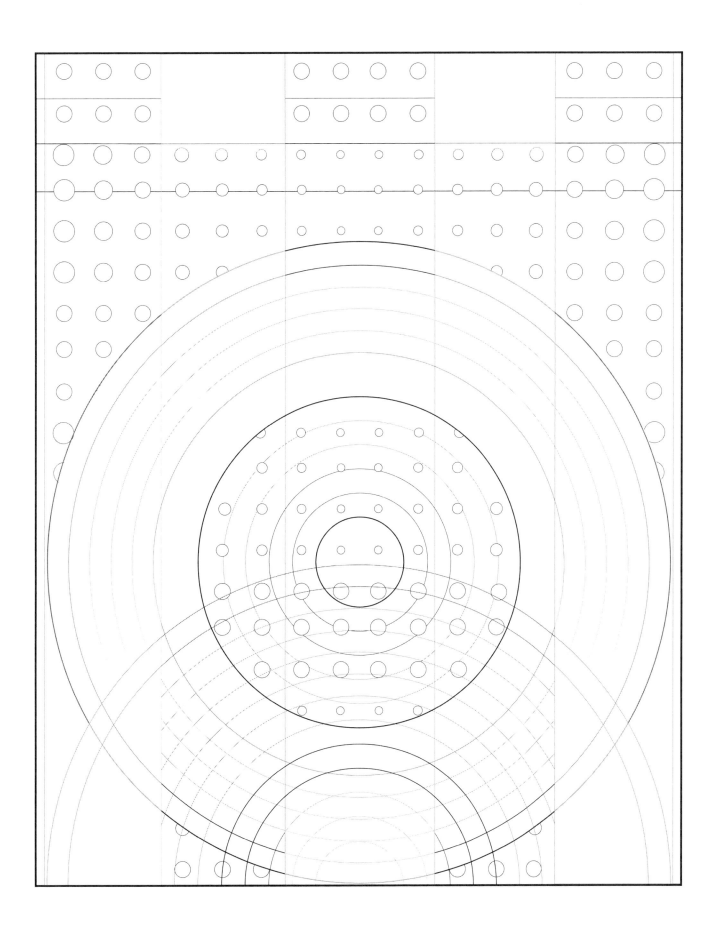

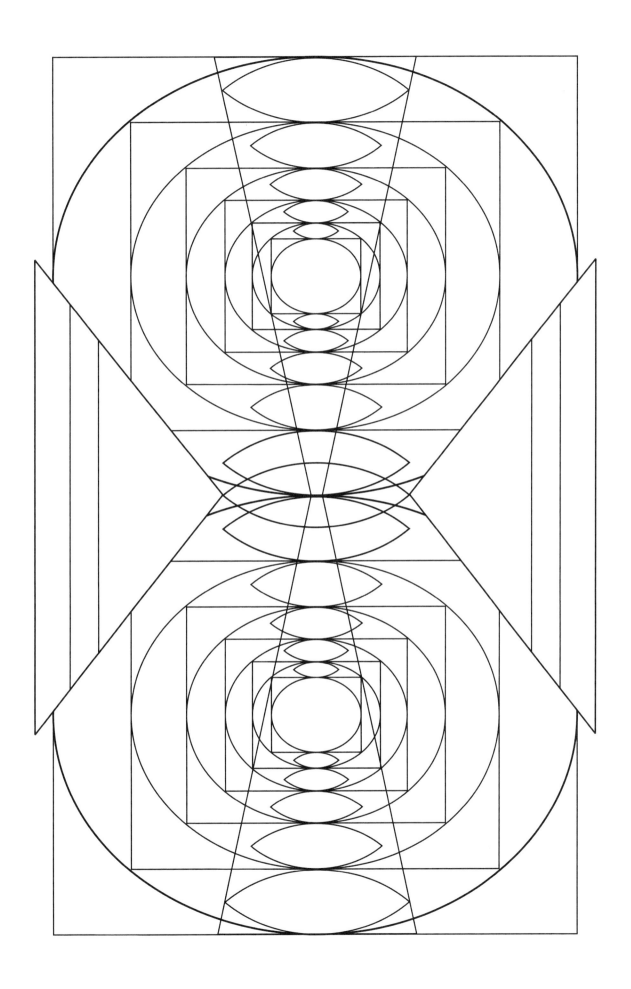

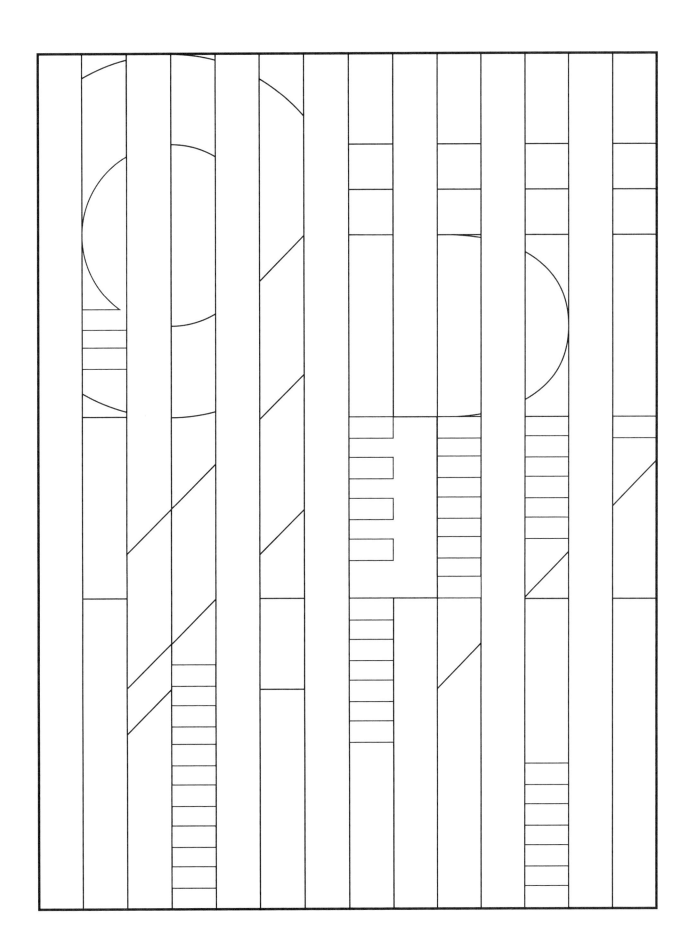

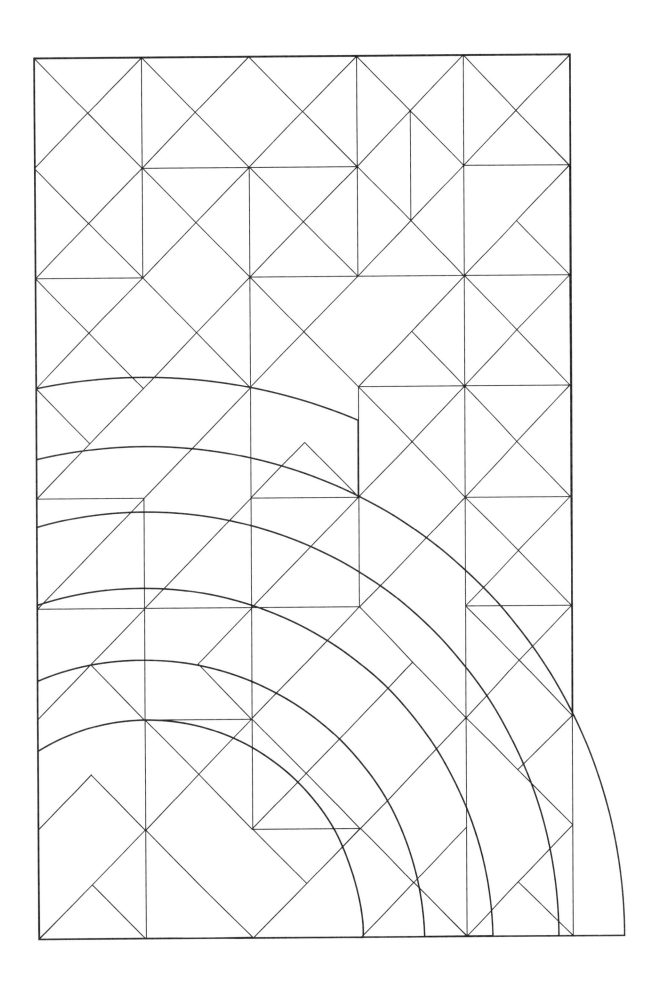

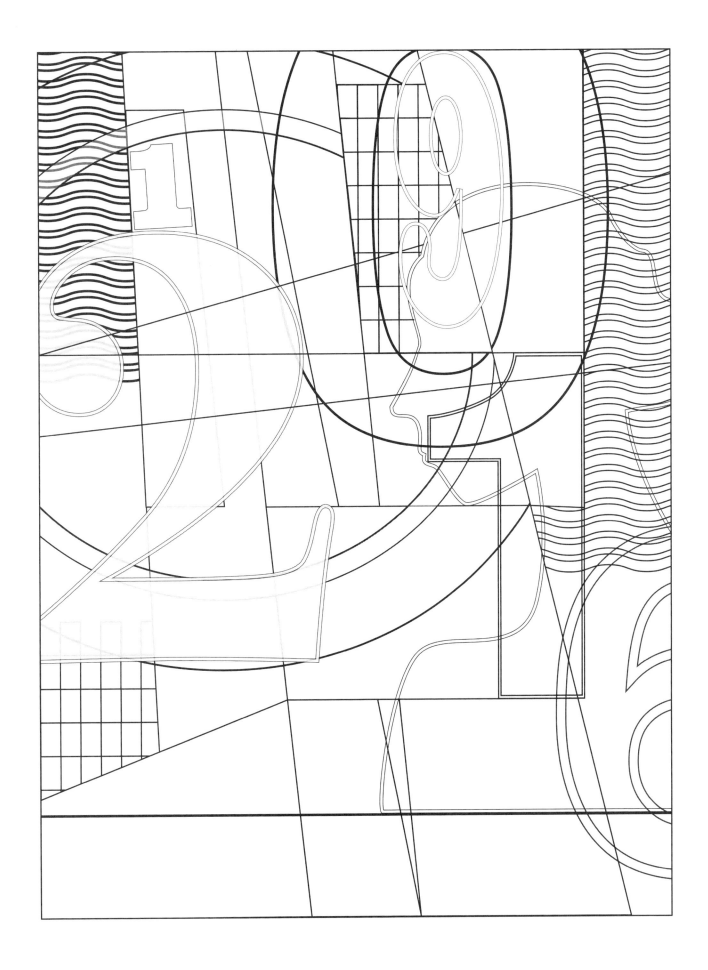

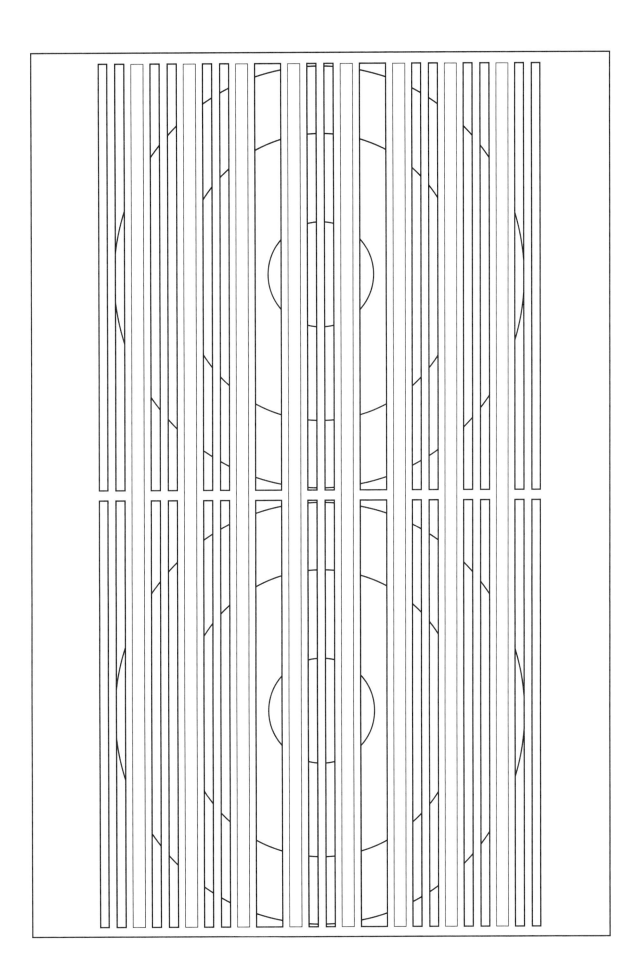

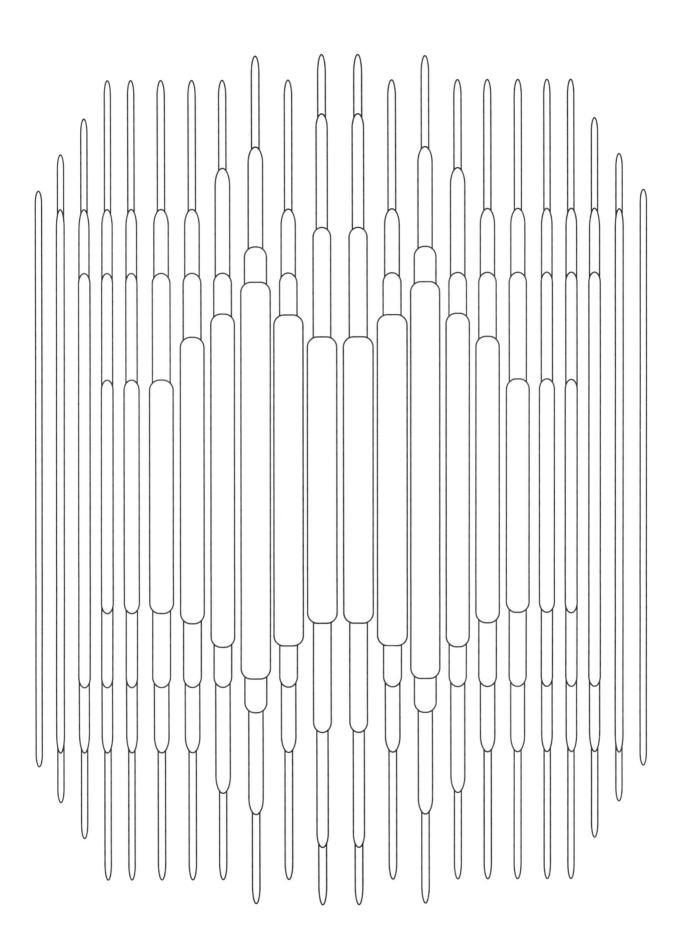

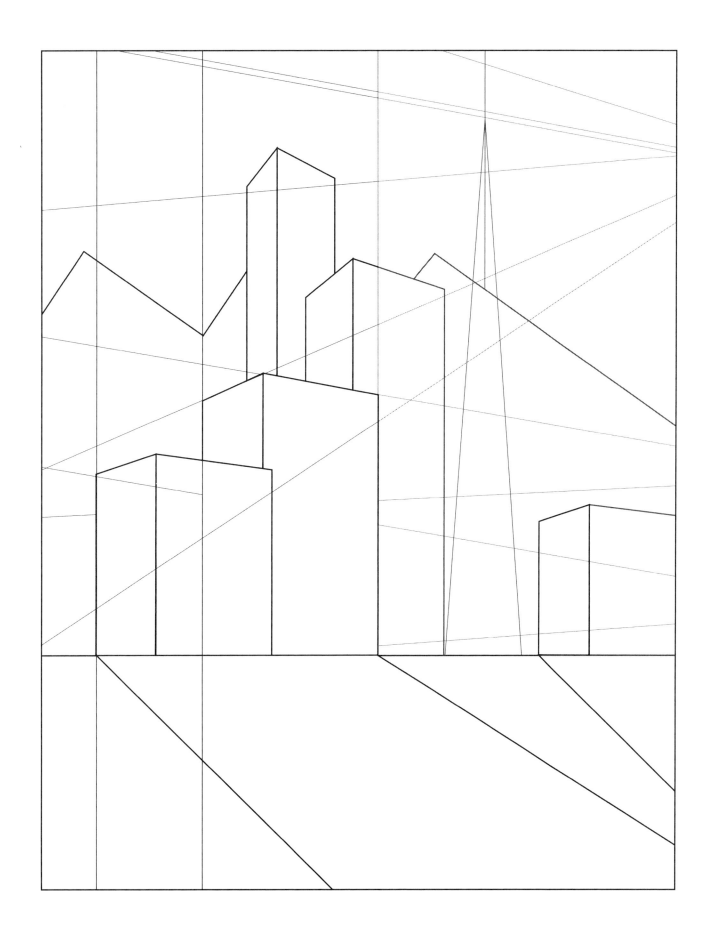

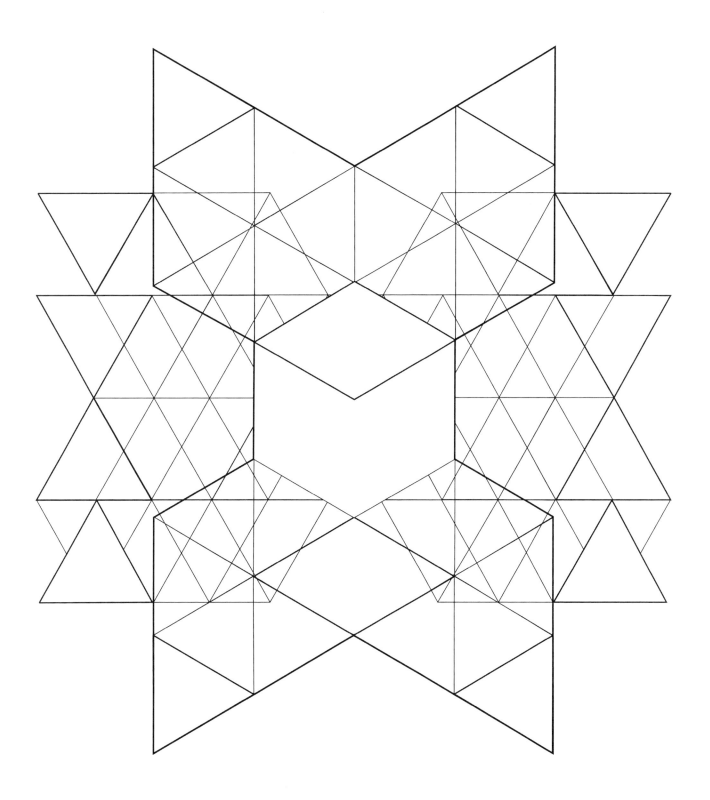

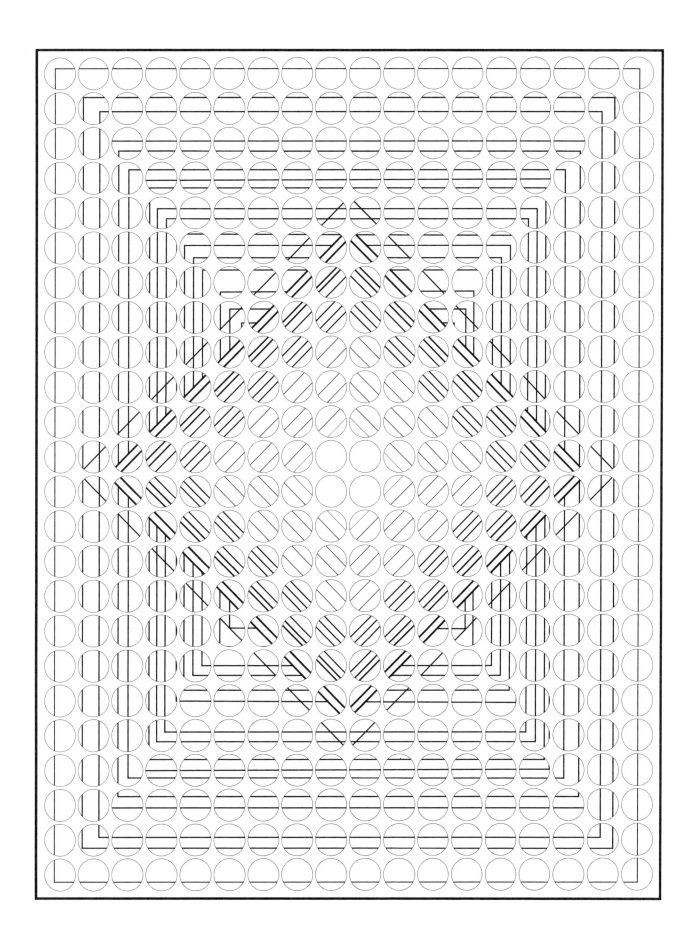

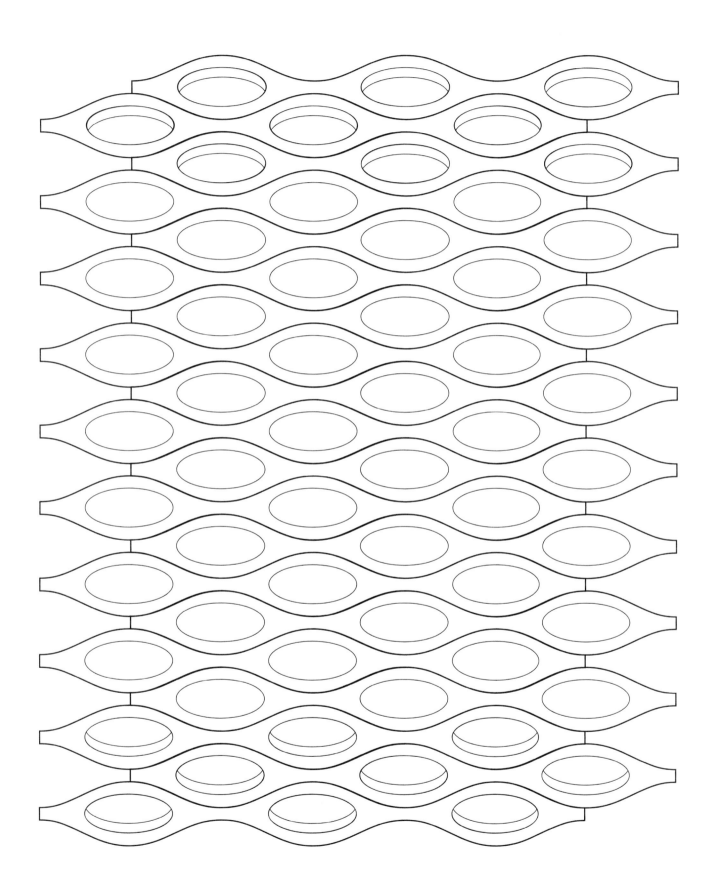

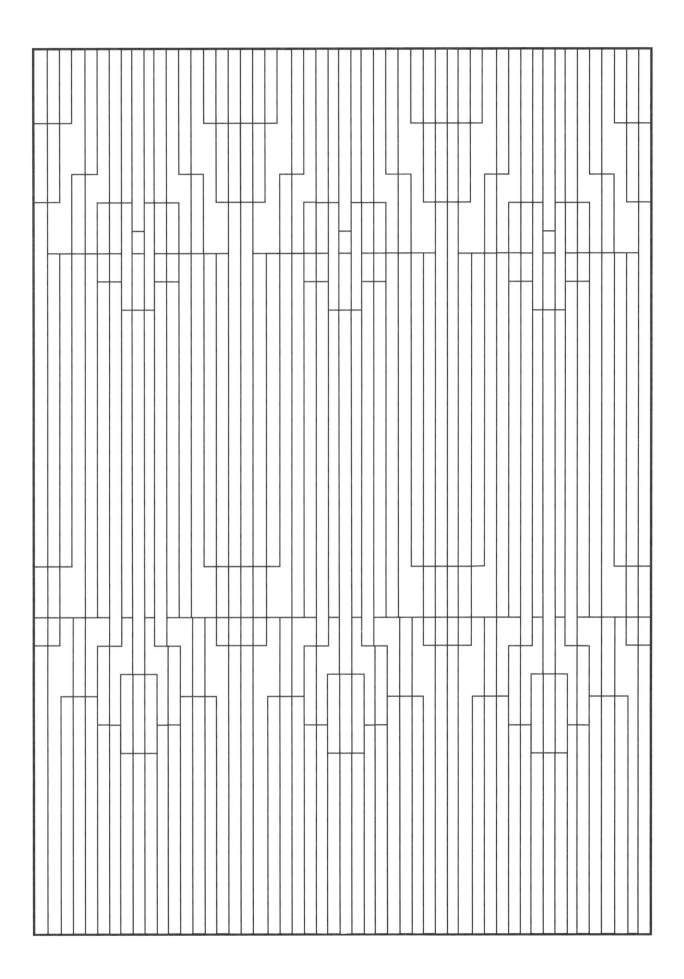

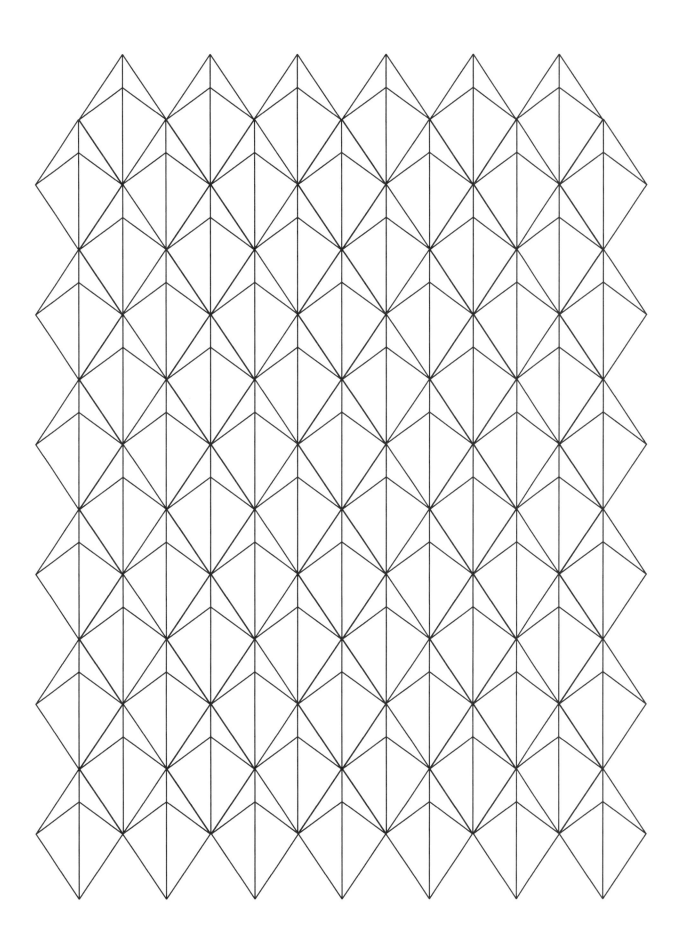

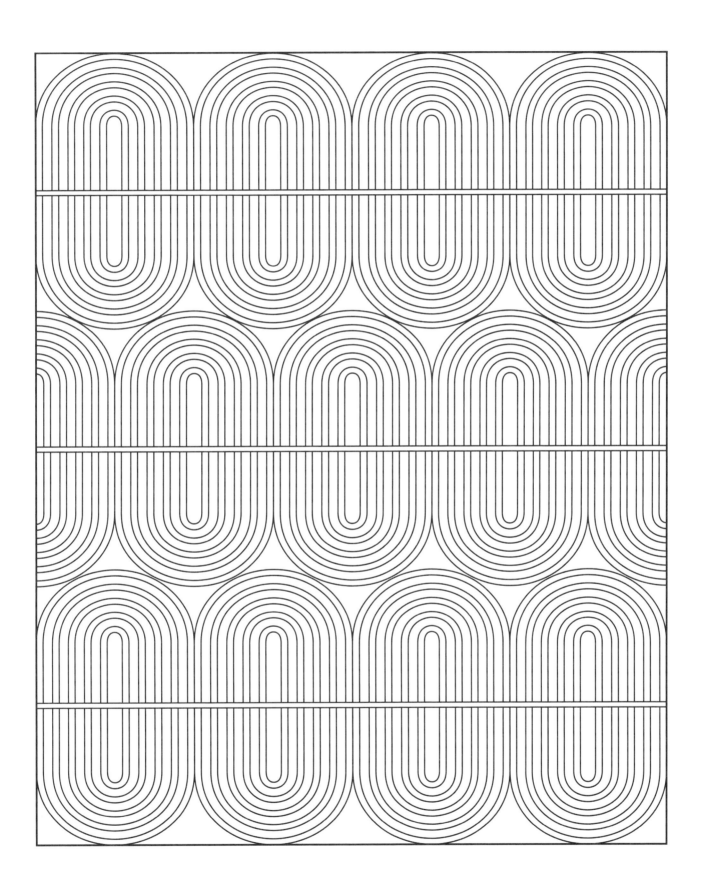

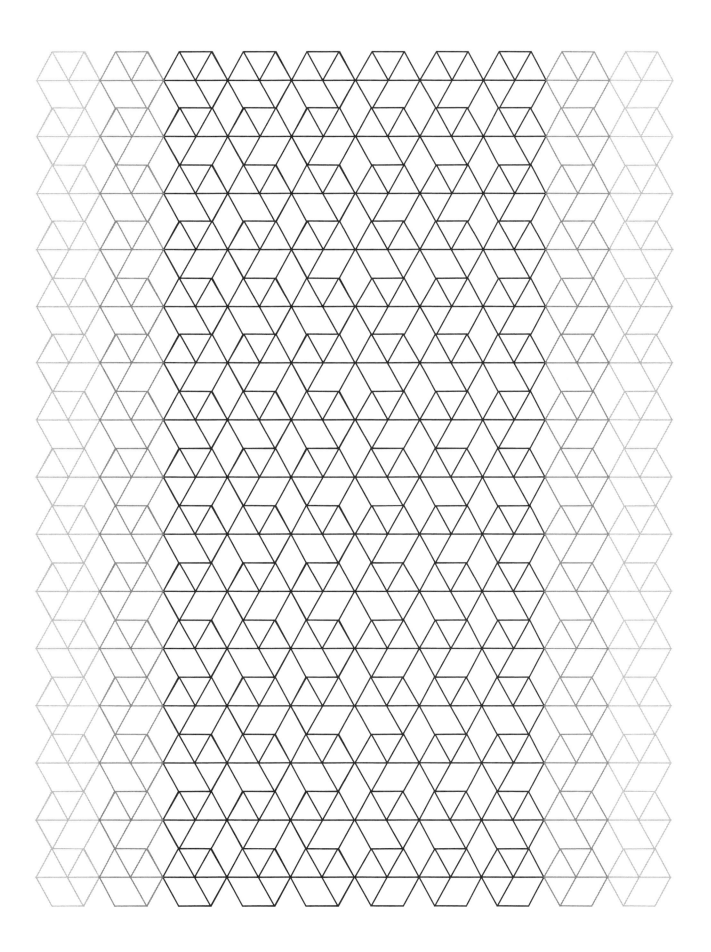

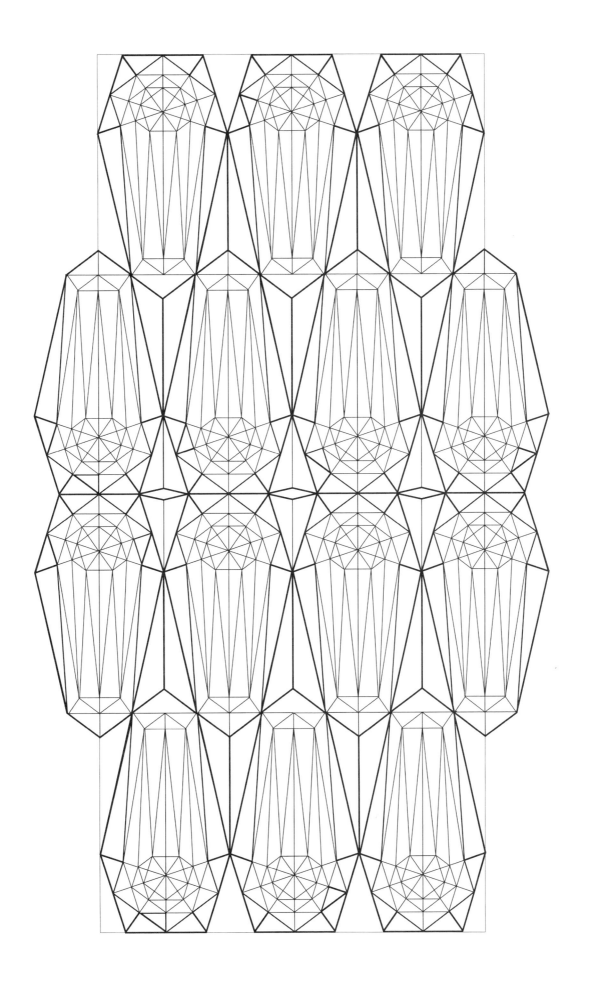

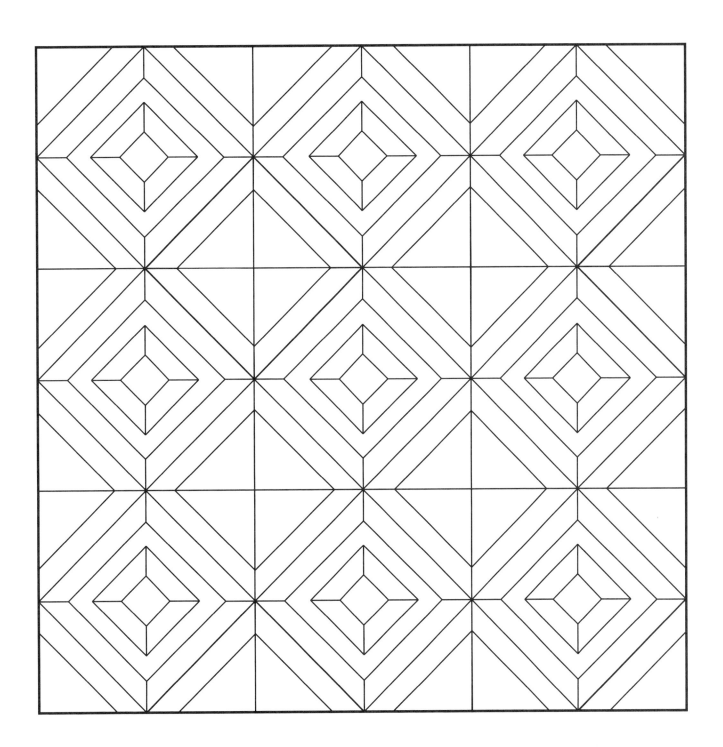

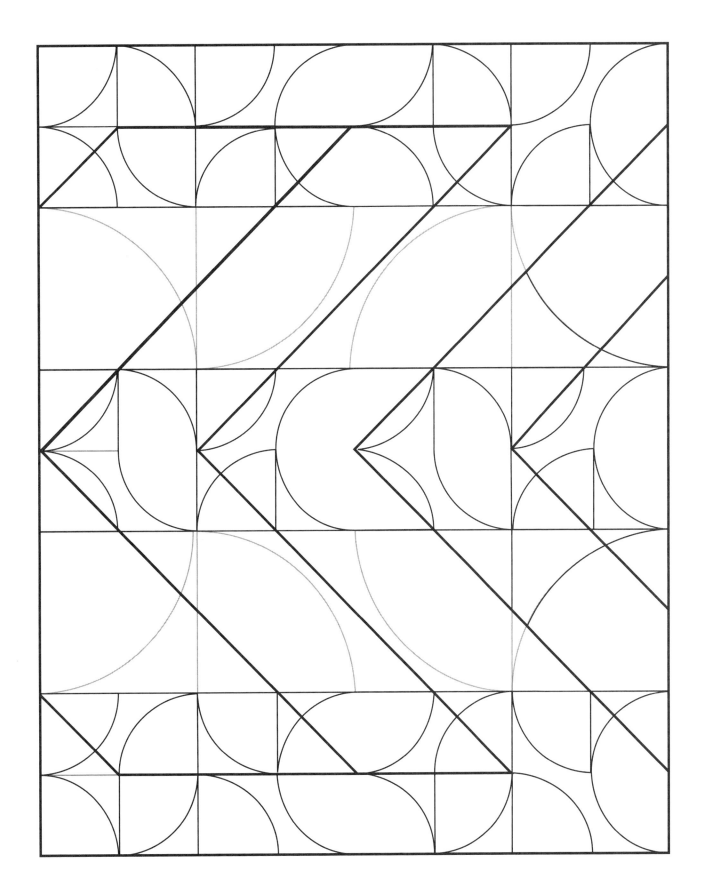

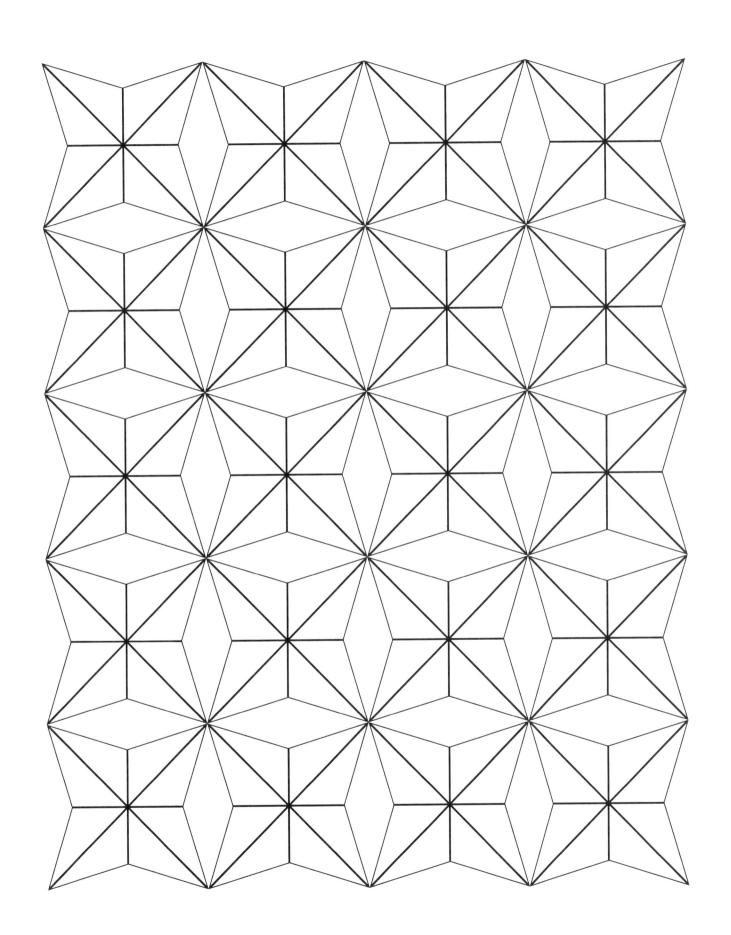

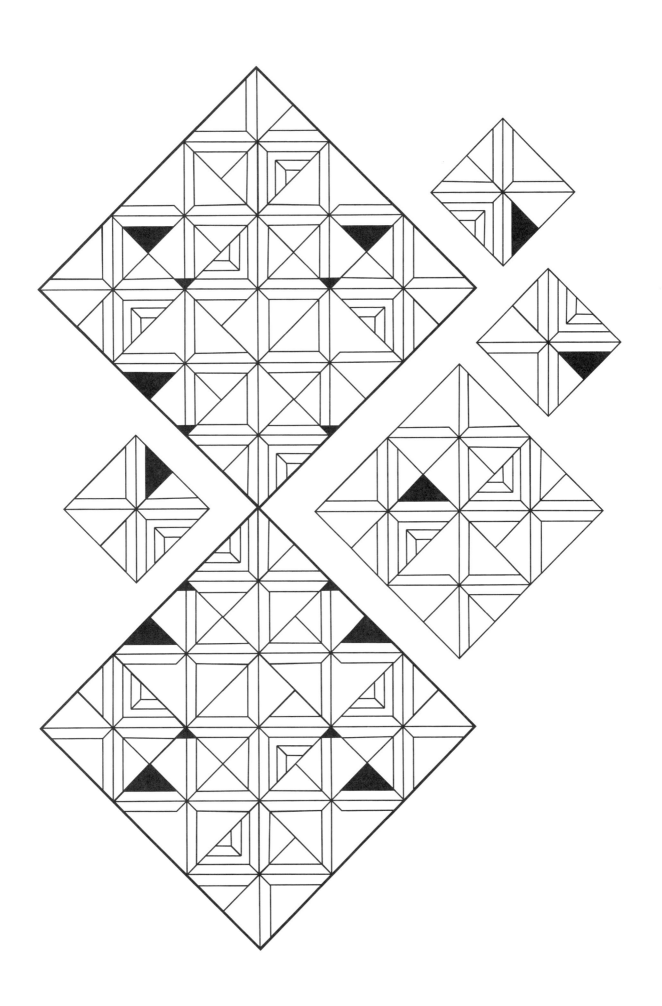

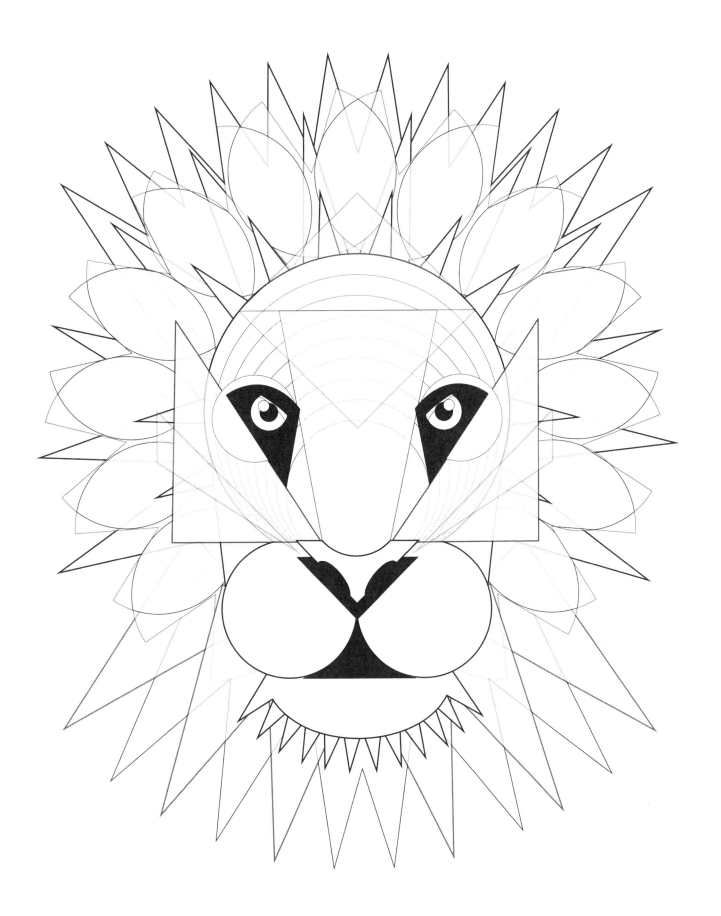

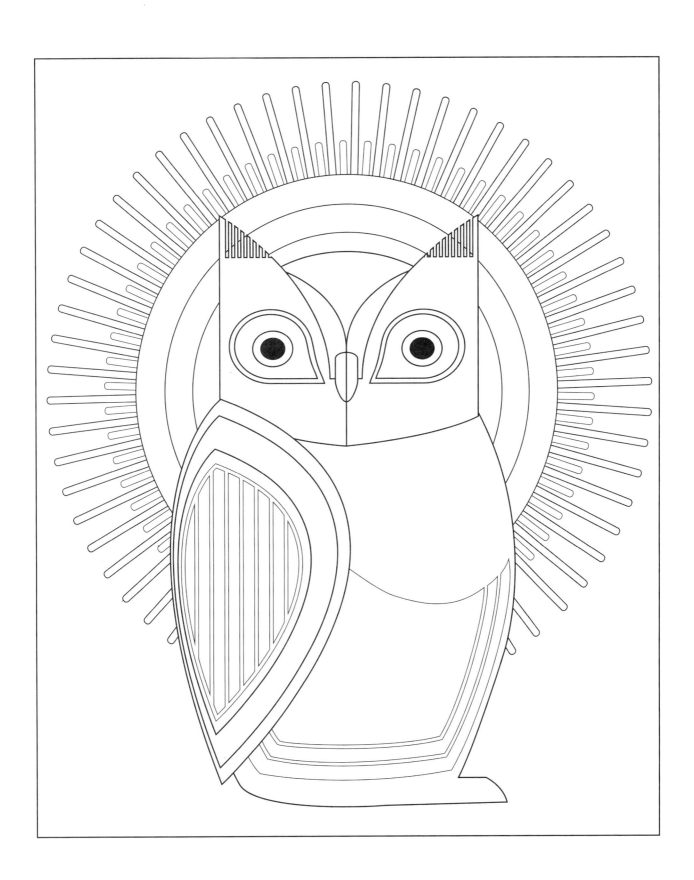

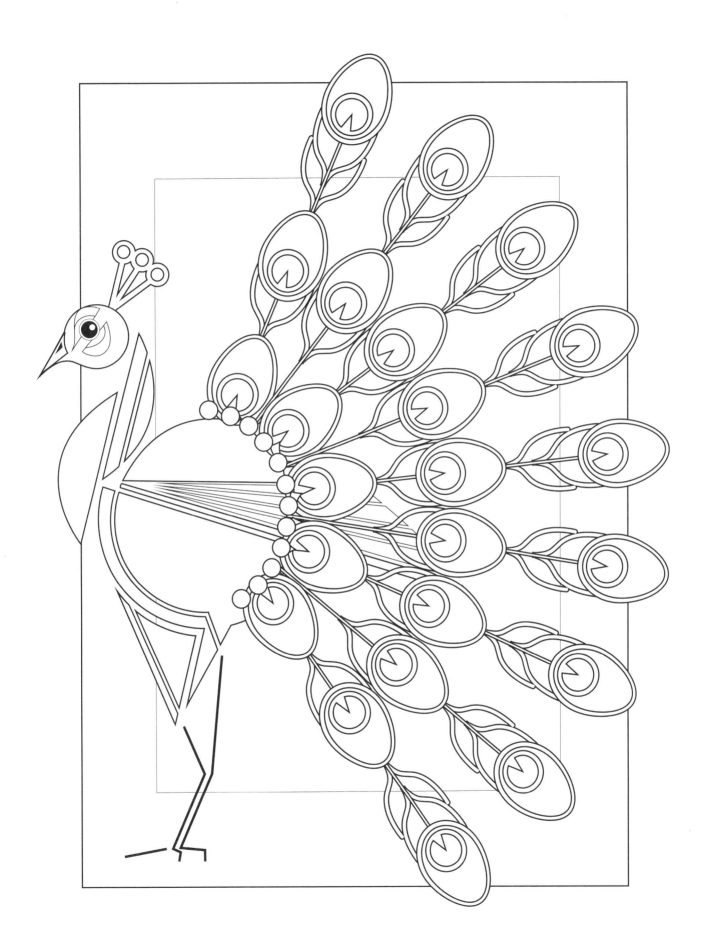

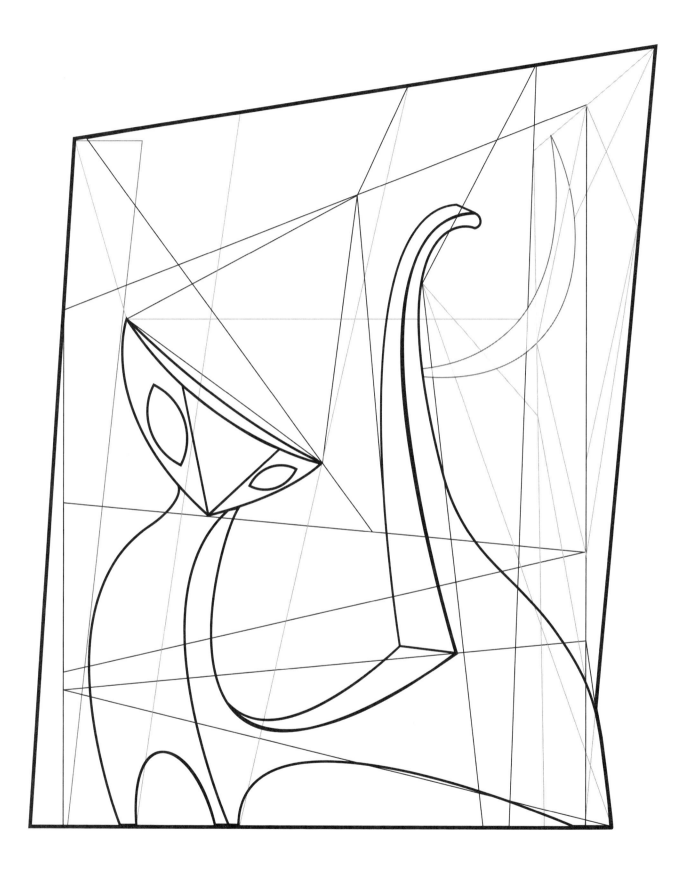

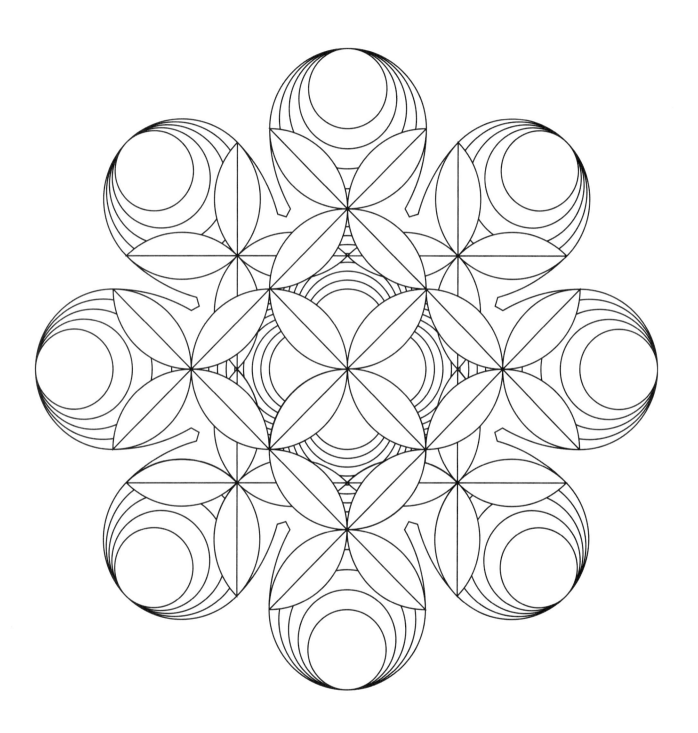

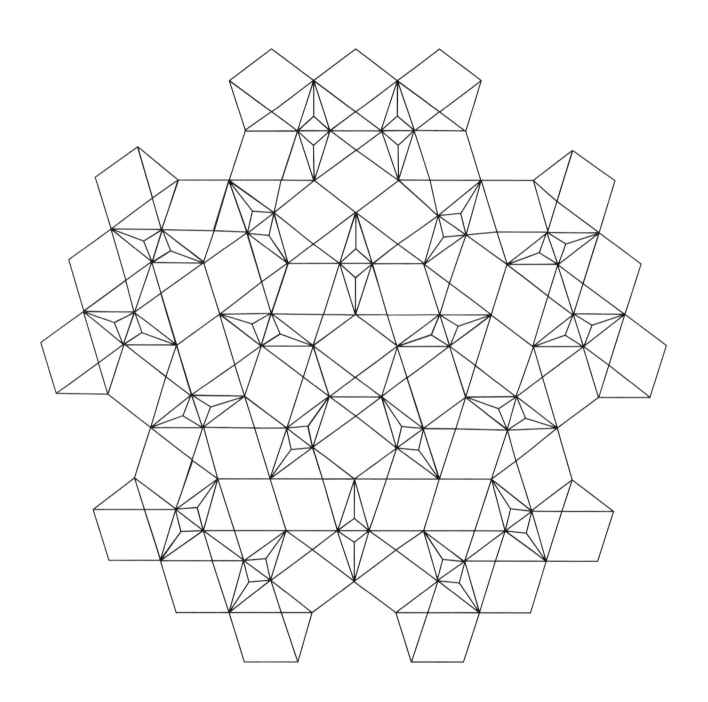

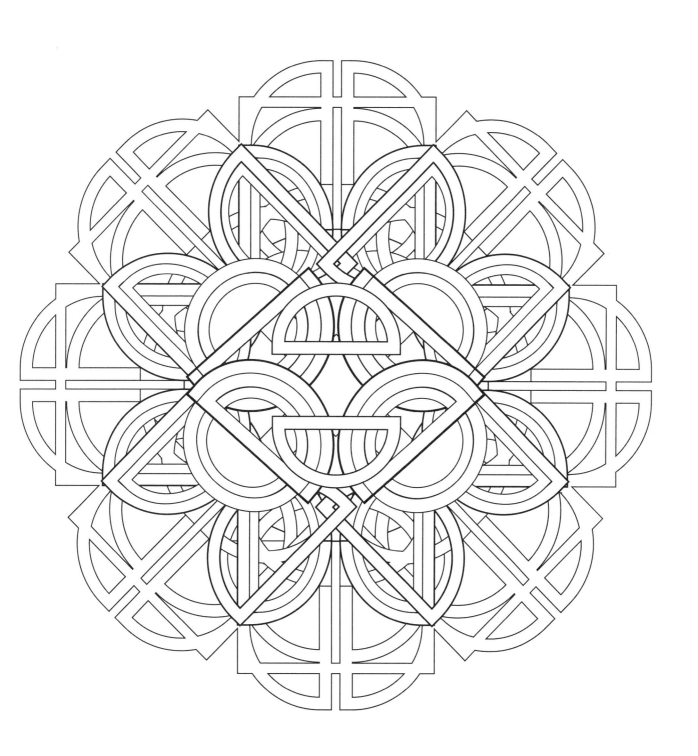

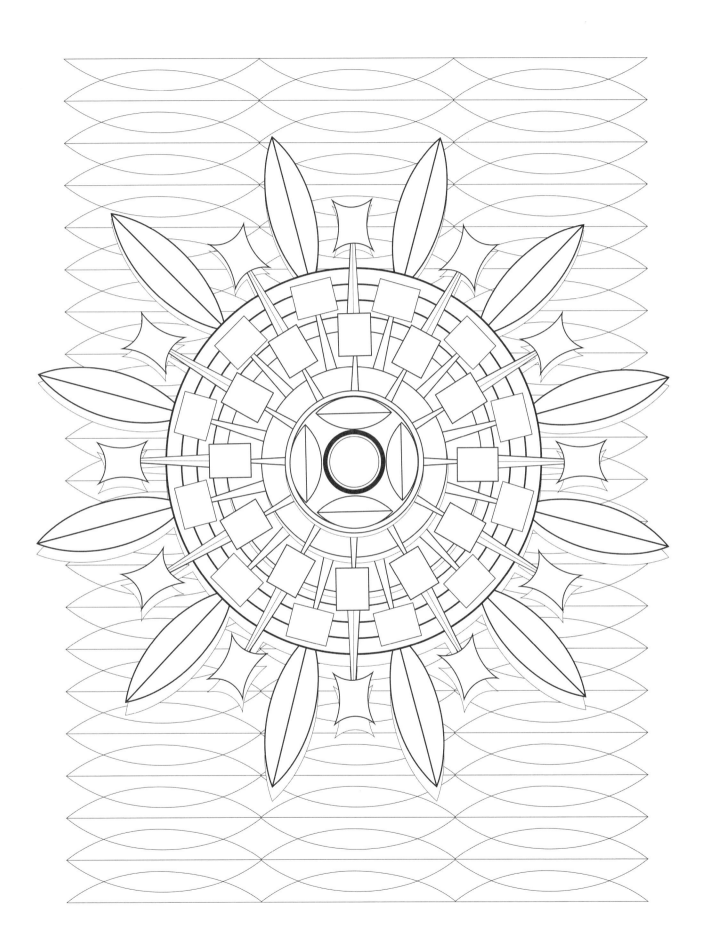

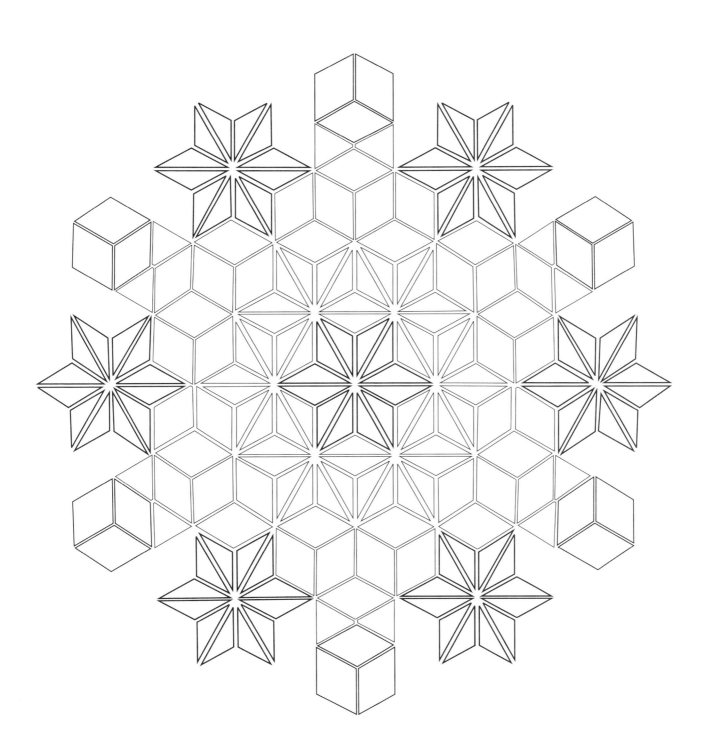

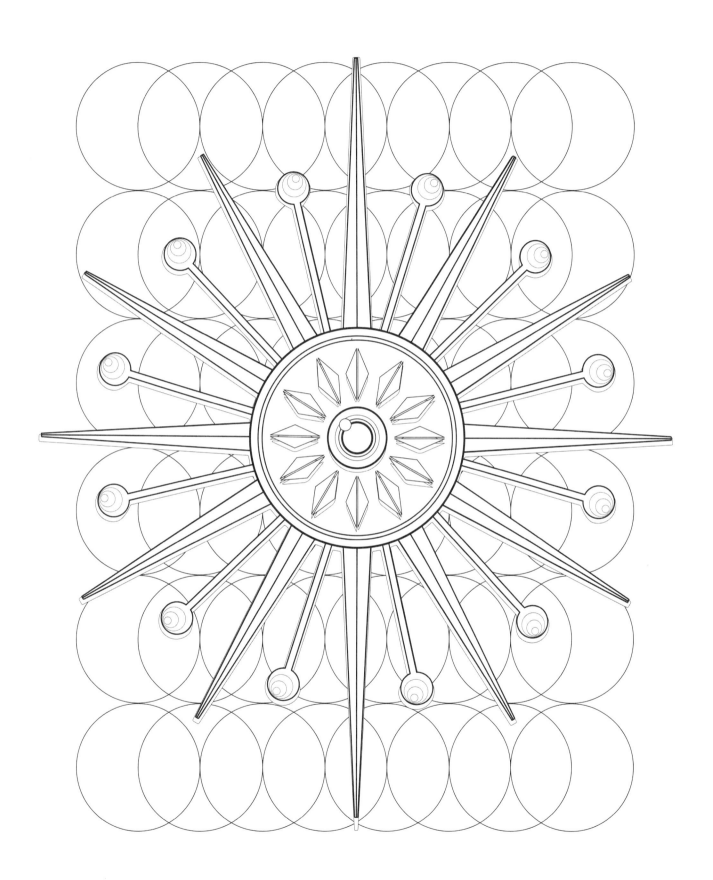

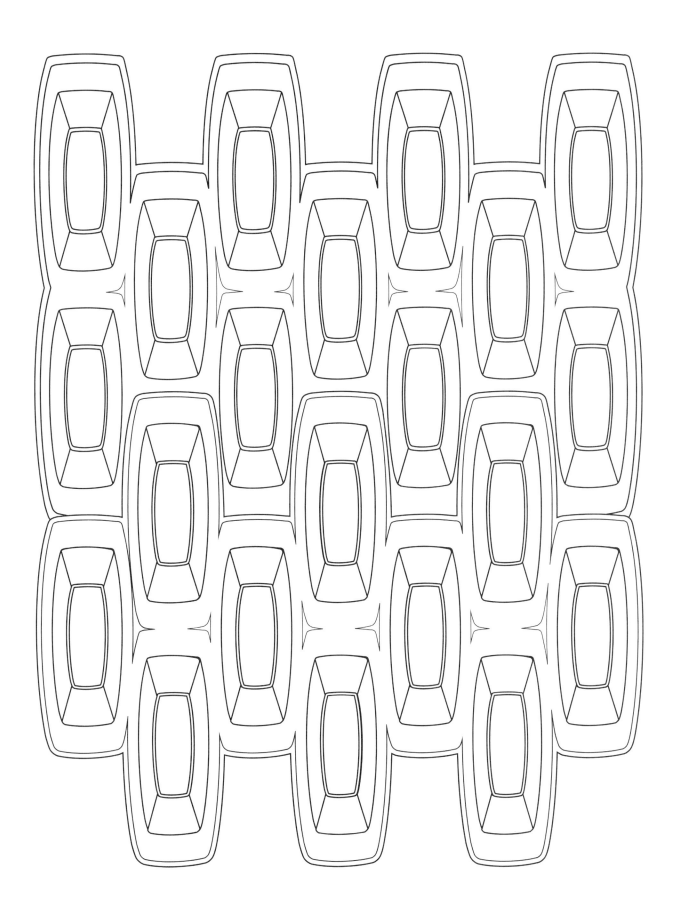

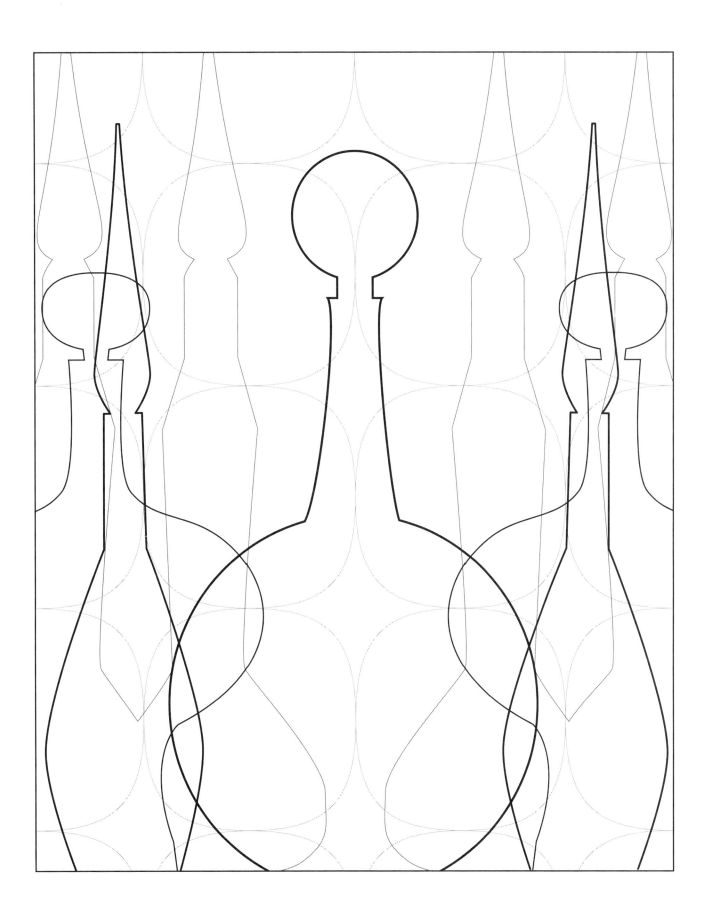

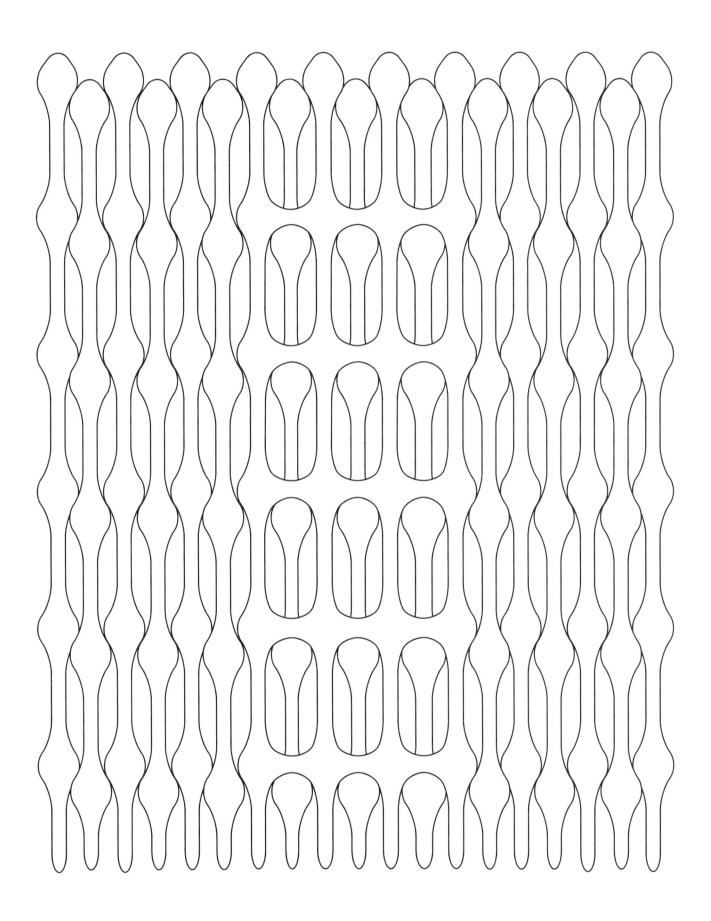

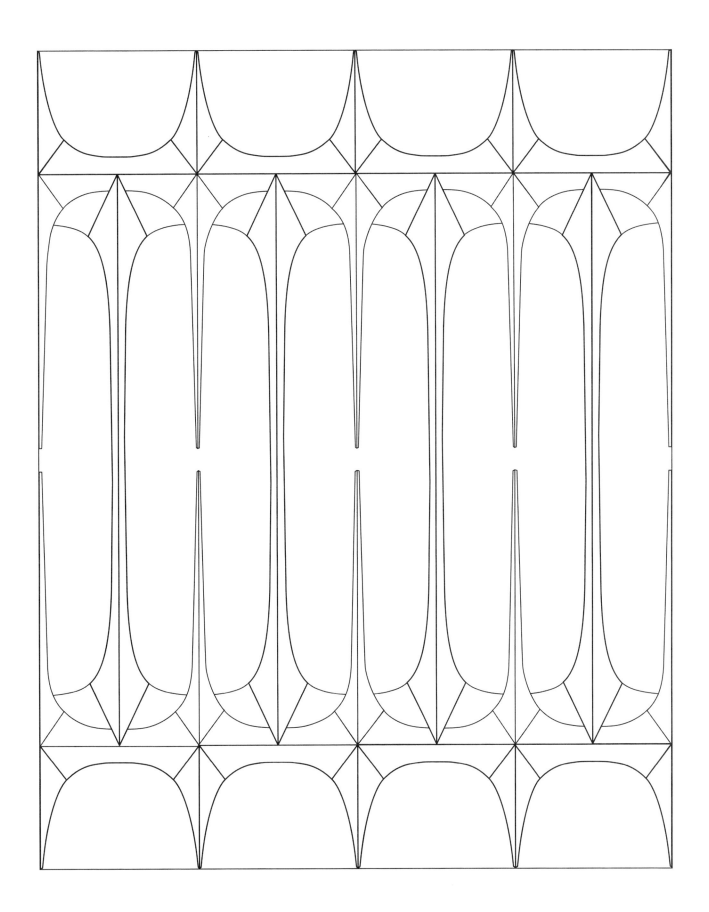

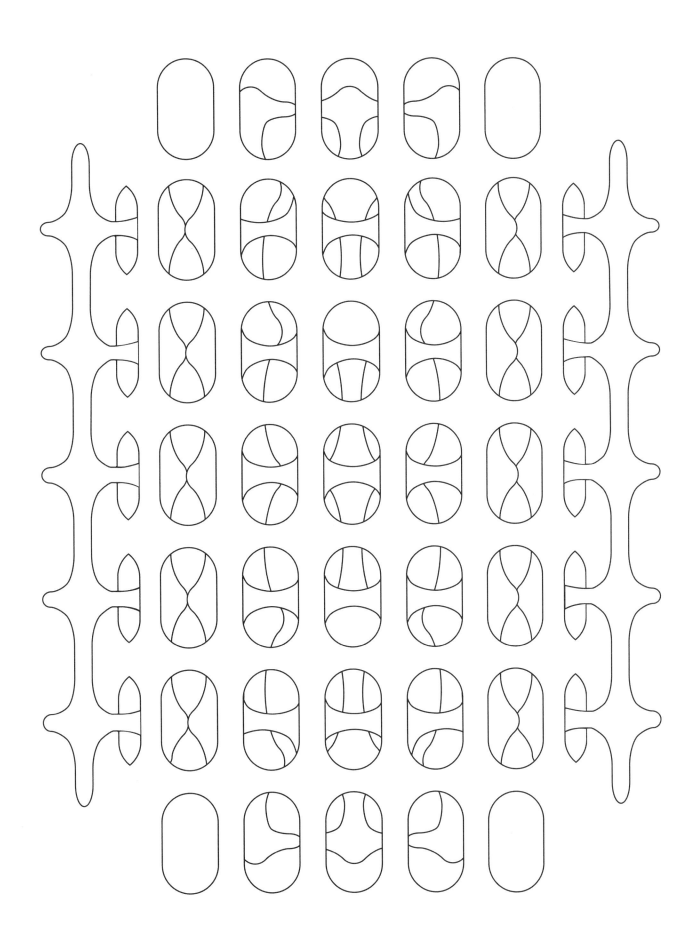

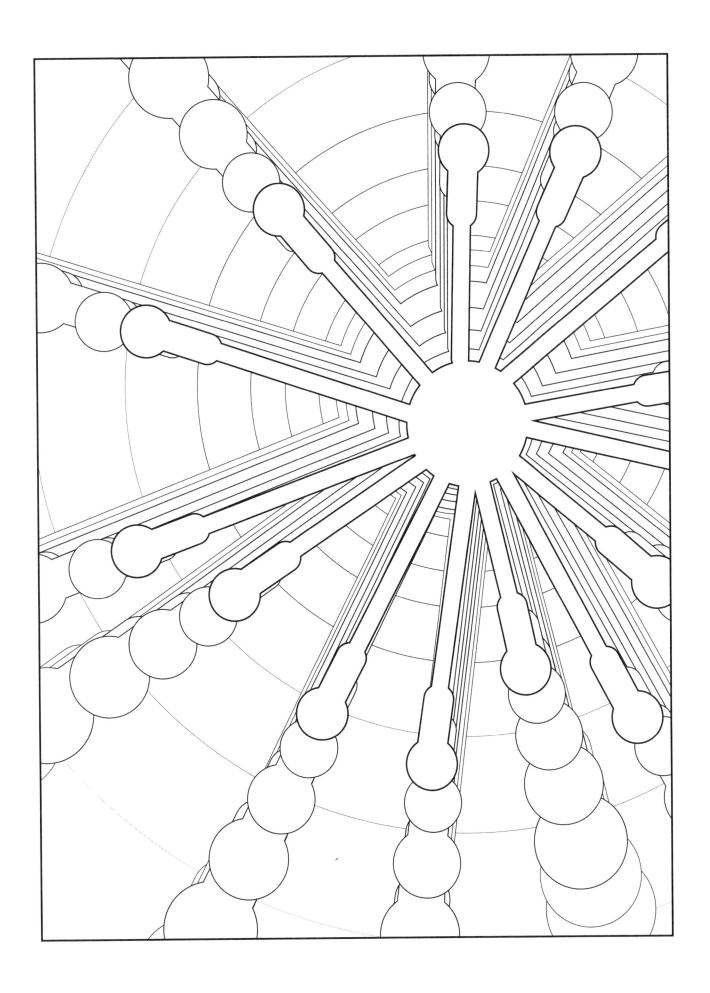

EXPERIMENT

EXPERIMENT

EXPERIMENT

EXPERIMENT